DOING
PLAYS
FOR A
ChangE

Maishe Maponya

DOING
PLAYS
FOR A
change

FIVE WORKS
INTRODUCED BY
IAN STEADMAN

MAISHE MAPONYA

 WITWATERSRAND UNIVERSITY PRESS

Witwatersrand University Press
1 Jan Smuts Avenue
Johannesburg
2001
South Africa

ISBN 1 86814 242 6

Applications to perform these works in public should be directed to Maishe Maponya, c/o School of Dramatic Art, University of the Witwatersrand, PO Wits 2050, South Africa.

Typeset, printed and bound by Kohler Carton and Print, Pinetown

Cover design by Sue Sandrock

Contents

FOR THE DISPOSSESSED

Before you get exhausted
In the lifelong ritual of struggle
Rekindle your dream by
Doing plays for a change
Let your children know
Where it all started.

Maishe
30 August 1994

Preface

Doing Plays for a Change marks the convergence of my thought-processes, creativity and activism as a playwright since the mid-1970s. I have engaged in a dialogue with myself for many years to rediscover myself and create my own consciousness to guide me through the milieu of contradictions. This collection emphasises this consciousness. In the process of writing and presenting the plays, I went through interesting experiences, some of which are included in the plays themselves, others of which have never been discussed with or known by the broader public. Not that these were unique experiences. Most writers, politically-conscious artists and activists can tell the same stories.

I conceived the idea of *The Hungry Earth* in 1978. After doing a few performances with my group Bahumutsi Drama Group at the Moravian Church Hall in Diepkloof, I was struck by a sudden sense of insecurity. The play astounded audiences who had not seen such heavily political work before and their response prompted me to send the script for legal advice. It went to the lawyer via Bishop Desmond Tutu, then General Secretary of the SACC.

In his reply to Bishop Tutu, attorney Raymond Tucker advised as follows: 'I am of the view that the play would constitute a contravention of the laws relating to racial incitement and the Publications Act and, in addition, the presentation would result in severe harassment of both the author and the performers' (Tucker R, 28 February 1978). He did not mention the title of the play in the letter. I assume that he did not want to compromise the group should the letter be intercepted.

I went to the homes of every member of the group and told them that the play was no more. I was not prepared to discuss the contents of the letter with them, except to tell them it was for their own safety.

A few months later I was discussing my progress in play writing with friends. During these discussions, my frustrations at having a play 'aborted at birth' emerged and I heard one of them mention the phrase 'publish and be damned'. That stuck in my mind and I went back to the members of the group to discuss the contents of the letter and told them that I was prepared to be 'damned' and that the play would go on if they were still committed to it. We had other performances organised but did not attract media attention. Journalists were rarely interested in coming to review plays in the townships.

Only one black female journalist from the banned *Post* had seen and reviewed my earlier play *Peace and Forgive* in 1977/8. About that work she had said: 'The place and the setting could be anywhere in the world of yesterday or today. The message is based on humanity – that suppression of one race by another is inhuman and cannot carry on forever' (*Post*, March 1978). For other journalists, if it was not Gibson Kente or Sam Mhangwane (the two writers who popularised township theatre in the 60s and 70s) it was not worth reviewing. I personally organised a symposium in the early 1980s at the Donaldson Orlando Community Centre (DOCC) in an attempt to discuss with journalists what could be done to improve the state of theatre in the township. None of them came. I remember trying to get one white journalist who worked for the *Rand Daily Mail* to come and review the production at the Moravian Church Hall. His response was that the majority of the readers of the newspaper were white and would not go into the township to see the play so there was no point in giving the production publicity.

Committed to seeing the play achieve its full potential, we booked the Box Theatre at the University of the Witwatersrand for three performances. Only one newspaper reviewed the production and recommended that I should either only direct or only act, not do both. The play could '. . . achieve its potential only through tightening up of the script but also with directing . . . the absence of a critical director is obvious' (*Voice Weekly*, April 1981).

I made arrangements with friends in the UK and Germany to organise performances for the group. Once we received an invitation to perform at community centres throughout the UK in 1981, we appealed for a sponsor. We advertised, but nobody was interested. Because we had to pay our own airfares from the guaranteed fees we would receive from each venue (£100) I decided to reduce the number of performers from five to three (of which I was one).

In response to the criticism from the *Voice*, I asked Ian Steadman to direct the play. We performed at the Battersea Arts Centre, Jackson's Lane Community Centre, The Inkworks (Bristol), Norwich Arts Centre, National Theatre (platform performance), Half Moon (London), Theatre Workshop (Edinburgh) and more than twenty others. From there we toured West Germany.

Among the media comments on our work was this one, from the *Evening Chronicle* in the UK: '. . . the play is not just a crying indictment of the politics, it is often wryly humorous. A little acid concealed among the flowers'. (July 1981)

It was during this first group tour abroad that I ditched my insecurities and fear of harassment of the performers. In an introduction to a pamphlet about the play published for the tour I wrote that:

The Hungry Earth emerges from the different aspects of our ill-fated lifespan. Through my eyes I have seen the devastations and drenching of my people into the wide-open mouths of this 'hungry earth'. I have heard them cry for mercy and I have seen them die many a time before those who fail to understand. We shall continue to punch with a clenched fist until the walls fall. (1981)

When the group returned from the tour, we performed at the Market Theatre and the media finally paid attention to us. Here is one example from a black journalist:

I felt a bit tired, as did perhaps also a few other theatre addicts who, like me, sacrificed JR and the entire Dallas gang for Maishe Maponya's *Hungry Earth* ... I say the play is explosive – not in its artistic content but in its protest eruption. (*Pace*, April 1982)

My next play, written in 1983, was *Umongikazi/The Nurse*. Bahumutsi Drama Group still had no sponsorship and I used part of my salary from Liberty Life Assurance Company for whom I worked to book the Laager at the Market Theatre. The play ran for three weeks. A week after that we performed at Glynn Thomas (Baragwanath Hospital). The morning after these performances, the security branch called at my home and left a note telling me to report to Protea police station the next morning at eight o'clock with the script of the play and my passport. It was two days before I responded and when I did I took a lawyer with me. I was told that this was going to be a 'friendly chat' and that I was not supposed to have brought my lawyer. I insisted that it was an interrogation.

I was asked about why I had written the play, where I got the material, and about my relationship with the Health Workers Association (HWA – now NEHAWU), its leadership and why we had organised performances at various hospitals and clinics. I was also asked what I hoped to achieve through the play.

The conditions in the health sector in South Africa were just as they were described in the play. I had spoken to nurses who had experienced these situations and to doctors (the HWA leadership) who confirmed the information. I did thorough research to inform my play because I believed that if the nurses (particularly) did not confront these situations they would continue to be pawns of the white management as represented by the South African Nursing Association (SANA).

The security branch policeman who was having a 'friendly chat' with me requested me to let him know should the HWA approach me to organise further performances. After the interrogation, I believed that I was being followed. I held several discussions with the HWA leadership and we agreed that we were only concerned about the security branch in relation to possible threats to members of the group.

Shortly before the play was due to tour Europe and the UK, the lead actress, Gcina Mhlophe was called to John Vorster Square police station. Her passport and mine were withdrawn, making it impossible for us to go with the group. I was not only the director but one of the four performers.

The organisers in Germany decided that the two actors should rework *The Hungry Earth* and perform that instead. The group, which received support and sympathy, used the refusal of our passports as publicity to pressurise the regime.

Thanks to the intervention of several foreign embassies, I was finally granted a passport, valid only for one month.

The premier of *Umongikazi* was due to take place at the Edinburgh Festival. Despite several assurances that Gcina's passport application was being reconsidered and that she might still be able to join the group, by opening night, she was still not with us and we asked Peggy Phango (of *King Kong* fame), a South African actress in exile, to take her role. She put up a brave performance, reading her words, and we supported her with our well-learnt lines and movements. The press never failed to capitalise on Gcina's passport refusal.

In a short review of the premiere, journalist Mario Relich wrote that the play was an 'occasionally uneasy but always absorbing mixture of hospital life depicted in a naturalistic manner, Ortonian black farce, or, rather white farce (actors in blonde wigs and red-haired masks) here, and Brechtian appeals to the audience.' (*The Scotsman*, 27 August, 1983)

Gcina Mhlophe only joined the group in the last two weeks of the tour after we had acquired the services of a Kenyan actress Wanjiku Kiarie, who gave inspired portrayals of Nyamezo.

In 1984 I started writing *Dirty Work*, a one-hander focusing on the regime's preoccupation with state security. Around the period of the writing, I was approached by novelist Nadine Gordimer to direct Beckett's *Catastrophe* for which she had acquired performance rights. I was excited by the proposal that I take charge of the work of this writer whose plays I had not read – in fact I heard the name for the first time from Ms Gordimer.

We arranged two readings of the play together to find meaning for ourselves. After the second reading, and having read the play a number of times on my own, I found it totally remote from my experiences as a black person living under apartheid. If there was any resemblance to my situation it was highly intellectual and would not appeal to black audiences who were being jolted by the direct agitprop theatre emerging from committed black writers and theatre makers.

In *Dirty Work*, I recreated the performance style of *Catastrophe* in which the Director (D) and his Female Assistant (A) use the Protagonist (P) as a puppet with no will of its own.

In *Gangsters*, the Protagonist is transformed into the poet, the Director is Major Whitebeard and the Assistant is Jonathan, a black security policeman. The idea of the poet was first inspired by my own experiences as a poet and performer but later found root in the image of Steve Biko, interrogated and tortured to death.

Gangsters and *Dirty Work* were written at the same time, informed and developed to a degree by Jon Maytham who played the original roles of Whitebeard and Piet Hannekom. Even now, it is rare to find a white performer directed by a black on the professional stages of South African theatre.

When *Gangsters* was restricted by the Publications Control Board to 'small, intimate avant-garde' theatres, it automatically meant that the play could not be seen by the majority of black audiences in the townships. There were no such theatres in the black areas in South Africa then and, even now, in the 'democratic' South Africa governed by a government of national unity, there are still none.

Jika, the least known of my plays, was workshopped with two actors from Uitenhage in the Eastern Cape. My intention was to create a play which would suggest ways in which poverty, squalor and political rhetoric could be eliminated.

In grappling with the philosophy of critical consciousness, I attempt to show practical ways to get my country out of the political and economic quagmire after the 'revolution'. Once I dreamt that 'revolution' was the only way to solve our problems, now a negotiated settlement is a reality. I am still asking, though, at whose expense that settlement was reached. I believe it is the duty of the writer to explore these issues and by doing plays for a change, to ensure that the oppressed do not remain oppressed. Re tla re re re ke dipitsi ra bona ka mebala (you can't tell a zebra but for its stripes)!

Maishe Maponya

Johannesburg, October 1994

THE THEATRE OF MAISHE MAPONYA

Ian Steadman

During the key apartheid years of the 1970s and 1980s, South African theatre practitioners attracted attention internationally with their uncompromising dramatisations of the evils of racial oligarchy. Throughout the 1970s and 1980s actors, directors, creative writers and theatre scholars purveyed to international audiences and readers theatrical images of the aspirations of South Africans affected by apartheid. As apartheid began to erode in the 1990s, theatre practitioners had to search for new targets and new methods, and much of the anti-apartheid theatre began to appear formulaic and dated. Nevertheless, the legacy of anti-apartheid theatre influenced post-apartheid theatre: the years of 'protest' and 'resistance' theatre bequeathed to later practitioners in the theatre a voice that was uniquely South African, and contemporary South African theatre cannot be understood without reference to the years of protest and resistance.

One of the prominent anti-apartheid theatre voices was that of Maishe Maponya.

Maponya was born in 1951, the son of a painter in the township of Alexandra adjacent to Johannesburg. When he was eleven years old the family was forcibly removed and resettled in Diepkloof, Soweto. Maponya began writing plays in 1975 when he was a clerk in one of South Africa's giant insurance companies, and the theatre offered him some relief from the routines of work in that institution. His writing career commenced in 1975 when he joined Medupi Writers Association which was later banned along with nineteen other organisations in October 1977. In 1977 he co-founded Bahumutsi Drama Group with whom he was later to produce most of his plays. In 1978 he co-founded the Allahpoets, a group of performance-poets, and wrote plays and poetry for performance in the townships.

His first play in 1976 was *The Cry*, which was written before 16 June, when Sowetan schoolchildren spearheaded one of the most important attacks on the apartheid state, and this was followed by *Peace and Forgive* in 1978, which was performed first in Soweto and later at The Market Theatre. In 1978 Maponya was the recipient of an award by the British Council and attended a course organised by the British Theatre Association in England. During this period he encountered Brecht's *The Measures Taken*. This play was a major influence in the writing of *The Hungry Earth*, Maponya's first prominent play, about labour and apartheid. *The Hungry Earth* was written in 1978 and revised and developed over the following few years. In 1982 Maponya wrote *Umongikazi/The Nurse*, about health conditions and the employment of nurses, and in 1984 he wrote the double-bill *Gangsters* and *Dirty Work* about detention and the security police. In 1986 he wrote *Jika*, a wide-ranging commentary on the possibilities and the failures of political liberation, and in 1987 he co-wrote with Amani Derrick Blackwood, a black British writer, *The Valley of the Blind*, a play about the Incas in South America.

Maponya has also written poetry and sketches and is highly regarded as a stage performer and director. In 1985 he was awarded the prestigious Standard Bank Young Artist Award for his contribution to South African theatre. Maponya holds the degree of MA from Leeds University and lectures in the School of Dramatic Art at the University of the Witwatersrand.

The Hungry Earth underwent numerous metamorphoses before it came to the attention of the theatre establishment in South Africa. It was first performed in May 1979 at the Donaldson Orlando Cultural Club in Soweto. Although it was rescripted and restructured on a number of occasions during 1979, in March 1980 it was presented in the form in which it would eventually be published (Maponya restructures his plays through the rehearsal process so that the script is often little more than the score of a performance created in workshop).

On 24 May 1981 *The Hungry Earth* left South Africa for a lengthy tour of Britain and Europe. As a Sowetan drama created by Maponya independently of white managements, it was invited to perform in community centres, universities and fringe theatres and also at the Edinburgh Festival, which it did to critical acclaim (see: *Newcastle Evening Chronicle* 8 July 1981, 'Fine Shades of Black'). It was considered in Britain as 'the other side of South African drama' (*Harlow Star* 23 July 1981). It was also invited to The National Theatre in London, where a platform performance was given at the Cottesloe Theatre in June 1981 (Johannesburg: *The Star* 'Tonight' 20 April 1981).

Invitations from further afield were frustrated by financial difficulties, but they included one to the USA and one to Nigeria (from Wole Soyinka). Eventually the play returned to South Africa where, having been acclaimed internationally, it was invited to The Market Theatre and was again praised by critics (*Rand Daily Mail* 'Showmail', 27 January 1982). The play toured to Germany again in May 1983 along with Maponya's new play *Umongikazi/*

The Nurse, and both works were enthusiastically received (*Theater Zeitung* nummer 59, Mai '83, Erlangen).

The Hungry Earth was originally intended for performance by five players, but just before the cast's departure for England, passport and financial difficulties necessitated a reorganisation of the play for three actors. The three-man format was subsequently retained, and Maponya toured the play with fellow actors Sydwell Yola and Dijo Tjabane. Maponya advertised the production on its British tour as a 'mirror and a voice of the dispossessed' (program for the British tour).

What is immediately apparent from a reading of *The Hungry Earth* is its Brechtian quality. It is (in many ways like the Brechtian *lehrstucke*) a didactic learning-play which demystifies black labour in South Africa. Maponya has said:

> The structure of my play is composed of a series of episodes that throw light on how apartheid came to be, and how it affects the black population of Africa.
>
> (Johannesburg: *The Star* 2 July 1981)

Maponya bases his play on the evils of the migrant labour system. His particular focus spreads further than the gold mining industry, however, and explores the network of associated socio-economic relations. The play appeared when South African historiography had already produced a significant number of studies showing the social, economic and cultural effects of the system of migrant labour at the time. Maponya's dramatisation of the social effects of migrant labour found resonance in the work of social scientists who revealed underdevelopment in the labour reserves of the rural periphery as a product of development in the South African industrial core: migrant labour was not seen as an isolated phenomenon but rather as a manifestation of a process of fundamental transformation in social life. This process became, in the 1970s, a major analytical focus of scholars interested in relations of capital in South Africa. The migrant labour system began to be interrogated by social scientists looking at the contradictory ideological, political and economic claims made by industry and the state. In the cultural sphere playwrights like Maponya set out to reveal the same issues by means of the theatre.

The theme is a fruitful one for theatre practitioners. The absence of sons and fathers from the rural areas led to social upheaval, marital breakdown with adverse side effects on children, demographic distortion, impoverishment of the rural areas, and the attendant effects of irregular capitalist development.

The effects of the system on the individual allowed Maponya to create a play which analyses both the political and personal consequences of migrant labour.

What is significant about the dramatic portrayal of these issues is the view from inside which theatre provides. As Brecht proclaimed, and as Maponya deliberately sets out to achieve, the theatrical representation of these issues can deal not only with the effects of a system on people, but also with the underlying motive causes – the structures of exploitation – which produce such effects.

The play consists of a choral prologue followed by episodic scenes. The locale is kept deliberately abstract so that the action and dialogue produce a number of different imaginatively created physical contexts. The few properties and elements of costume used are deposited by the actors in piles on the perimeter of the stage when they are not in use. The stark theatricalism of the play is evident from the very first moments in performance: from a darkened auditorium emerges the sound of a single voice singing in the vernacular. The song, translated as:

> Wake up mother Africa . . .
> Wake up . . .
> Before the white man rapes you

is a melancholic, slow invocation which takes place in complete darkness, the voice drawing nearer while the actors take their positions on stage. As the song ends the lights snap up to reveal the actors facing the audience. They speak in unison, inviting the audience to join in a journey with the Bahumutsi Drama Group.

The action of the play is then structured into brief scenes – the Hostel, the Plantation, the Train, the Mine and then the Mining Compound – through which Maponya pursues his theme.

Maponya's script for the play underwent numerous changes before its publication. The final published text is merely an edited scenario of quite spectacular action. In much of the performance, word and gesture are deliberately linked in political icons. The actors deliberately over-emphasise through gestic language the symbolic importance of phrases like 'We will fight hard' and 'We will rise up', by raising clenched fists high in black power salutes. This leaves the audiences in no doubt as to the political dimensions of the performance.

The unifying energy of such gestic language is central to Maponya's intentions. Unconcerned with three-dimensionality in his characterisation, he presents stereotypes in stock situations. Indeed, the actors in Maponya's dramatised social commentary depict functions rather than characters. He has structured his action to develop the story from historical antecedents, through a description of rural plantation labour, to a portrayal of migrant labour – and he draws his theme to a focus on the central cog in South African industry, showing apartheid as a servant of capital. In all of this the underlying theme in performance is political resistance and the call to 'rise up' in rejection of the oppressive state.

Maponya's acknowledged Brechtian style is the most prominent feature of the dramaturgy and is also the key to understanding the ideological basis of the play. The Brechtian influence is apparent not only in the formal aspects of the play, but also in the vision inscribed therein – a view of theatre as political demystification. Following Brecht, Maponya holds that the ideological function of theatre is its most significant feature. Like Brecht, he tries to use theatre to demystify the political and economic relations of social life. By presenting dynamic images of black working-class life, Maponya tries to expose the contradictions of the migrant labour system. In line with the Brechtian aesthetic, Maponya does not concern himself with the moral or psychological complexities of individual characters, but concerns himself rather with themes which affect the black working class in general.

By the time Maponya returned to South Africa after a successful European tour of *The Hungry Earth*, black theatre was beginning to assert an identity in the established theatre venues on the Witwatersrand. The Market Theatre had become a recognised 'home' for black playwrights. Maponya himself, increasingly forced away from the townships by the difficulties of censorship and bureaucratic control of halls by government authorities, turned his attention to institutions like The Market Theatre. The Market was at this time beginning to achieve international success through the presentation of a number of superbly crafted plays. Although Fugard's *Master Harold . . . and the Boys* opened firstly in the USA, it was the Market production which was chosen to play at Britain's National Theatre. *Woza Albert*, created out of improvisation by Barney Simon, Percy Mtwa and Mbongeni Ngema, created a sensation with its theatrical demonstration of the realities of black experience in South Africa in the 1980s.

Maponya wrote *Umongikazi* in 1982. Locating his play within contemporary debates about union activity amongst health workers (debates which gave rise to the National Education Health and Allied Workers Union), and basing his story on real events, he wrote in this play about the practices and effects of racism in health services in the country. The play depicts events at Baragwanath

Hospital, claimed to be the largest hospital in the southern hemisphere. Maponya portrays the working conditions of nurses and the acts of intimidation faced by them. He had planned a country-wide tour of the play, intending to perform the piece in clinics and hospitals, but he encountered massive bureaucratic interference and harassment. As with *The Hungry Earth*, he was forced to cancel performances because of harassment (which included interrogation by Security Police about Maponya's involvement with health workers). When he took the play abroad similar harassment occurred, with Maponya and his leading actress initially being refused passports, but finally overcoming the problems to engage in another successful international tour.

Once again, as in *The Hungry Earth*, Maponya creates in *Umongikazi* a theme of political resistance which serves as a backdrop for the action of the play. The theme is manifest in the form of a song which emphasises a call to arms to resist the impositions of the apartheid state. The play is a collage of scenes revealing the day-to-day harassment of nurses and the intimidatory actions of corrupt officials and oppressive police, and concludes with a rousing call for a union and solidarity against the oppressor.

> ... it was the closing song sung in Xhosa that made my skin crawl and cast its spell on the black members of the audience. It was a moving call to the oppressed to arise and awake from their slumbers because the rays of the first sun of the new dawn were upon us ...
>
> (Don Mattera: *The Star* 'Tonight' 10 January 1983: 'Maponya dramatises a bitter message')

By the mid-1980s South Africa was ruled by an oppressive bureaucracy based on a conception of national security. As Maponya wrote his next plays *Dirty Work* and *Gangsters* the police and army maintained a tense vigil in the townships. It was a period when many people were detained, murdered, harassed and assaulted. On 20 August 1983 twelve thousand people gathered in Cape Town to launch the United Democratic Front – an organisation which linked trade unions, community groups and other bodies who were united in opposition to the government's constitutional proposals to entrench white dominance and exclude Africans.

Violent resistance marked the government's implementation in the second half of 1984 of a constitutional system which entrenched white domination, gave nominal representation to coloureds and Indians, but excluded direct participation by Africans. Apart from demonstrations and pickets calling for a boycott of the new constitution, there was an escalation in the war against apartheid in the form of increased sabotage and underground resistance activity. This violent resistance caused the militarisation of South African society and an intensification of repressive measures used by the state Security Police, in a reversal of the more strategic policy dictated by 'constructive engagement'.

Maponya, building on his previous work, was one of the many playwrights responding to these political developments. He presented *Gangsters* at The Market Theatre in the second half of 1984, on the eve of an outbreak of violence in the townships which continued sporadically throughout 1984 and into 1985. Both plays dealt with aspects of South Africa's network of security and control. In *Dirty Work*, a satirical view of the paranoia of a white security official, he presented a humorous prelude to aspects of detention and prevention by South African police, which he explores in more serious vein in *Gangsters*.

In 1984 the theme of detention and control was pertinent indeed. At the time South Africa experienced a peak of detentions and bannings not witnessed since 1973, the height of the Black Consciousness movement. Banning orders were issued in terms of the Internal Security Act 74 of 1982, the successor, via numerous amendments, to the Suppression of Communism Act of 1950. Whereas the 1950 Act applied only to actions which could (broadly) be seen as supporting 'communism', the 1982 Act applied to actions which might endanger 'security' or 'public order'.

A notorious 'detention clause' allowed the Minister of Justice to detain people in order to prevent them from engaging in activities which either furthered the cause of communism or endangered the safety of the state or the maintenance of public order. This clause was invoked frequently. In addition, the Minister could detain witnesses for as long as it took for a trial to be concluded. It is clear therefore that the phenomenon of detention enabled the state ruthlessly to control opposition.

Section 5 (1) of the Internal Security Act is of special interest. This section provided that if the Minister was satisfied that any publication:

(a) Serves inter alia as a means of expressing views or conveying information the publication of which is calculated to endanger the security of the State or the maintenance of law and order;

(b) professes, by its name or otherwise, to be a publication for propagating the principles or promoting the spread of communism;

(c) serves inter alia as a means for expressing views or conveying information the publication of which is calculated to further the achievement or any of the objects of communism;

(d) is published or disseminated by, or under the direction or guidance of, an organisation which has been declared an unlawful organisation . . .;

(e) serves inter alia as a means for expressing views propagated by an organisation referred to in paragraph (d) . . .;

(f) serves inter alia as a means for expressing views or conveying information the publication of which is calculated to cause, encourage or foment feelings of hostility between different population groups or parts of population groups of the Republic . . .'

(Internal Security Act 74 of 1982)

he could prohibit the publication or its dissemination.

The other Act which is of particular significance to an understanding of *Gangsters* is the Publications Act (42) of 1974. This was the successor to the Publications and Entertainments Act of 1963. Any publication or performance which the Publications Control Board deemed 'undesirable' was subject to censorship or banning.

Dirty Work requires little commentary: it is a monologue reflecting the paranoia, the malice, and the foibles of a security official, and it provides an interesting curtain-raiser to Maponya's thematic concerns in *Gangsters*. In the first version of the latter play Maponya drew liberally on the play by Samuel Beckett, *Catastrophe* (Paris, 1982), to explore the themes of power and alienation, and make them relevant to the South African context. In the version of *Gangsters* published in this volume he has extensively revised the play and focuses on the spirit of resistance of artists working under repressive conditions. There are three characters in the play. The 'gangsters' of the title are the two security policemen Major Whitebeard (a white security chief) and Jonathan (a black policeman). Masechaba, a black woman poet, is the third character (in the original production, named Rasechaba, a man, and played by Maponya).

There is no small irony in the theme of the artist's resistance to oppression in this play by Maponya. Having himself suffered at the hands of interrogators early on in his career as a writer, Maponya then experienced different forms of harassment after recognition as a playwright had brought him a high-profile professional career in the theatre.

On 9 August 1984 Mannie Manim, the Managing Trustee of The Market Theatre, received a letter from the Directorate of Publications in Cape Town. The letter is worth quoting in full:

Dear Mr Manim

PUBLICATIONS ACT, 1974: PUBLIC ENTERTAINMENT: 'DIRTY WORK/GANGSTERS'

This is to inform you that a Committee of Publications appointed under section 4 of the above Act has viewed the above play, as performed at the Market Laager Theatre and decided as follows, as provided for in section 30:

1. The play 'Dirty Work' is approved unconditionally.
2. In regard to the play 'Gangsters' –

(a) it may only be performed in small intimate fourwall theatres, of the experimental or avant guard [sic] type;
(b) a request for approval of any future venue for the performance of the play must be directed via the Directorate of Publications;
(c) the Laager Theatre in the Market Theatre complex in Johannesburg is an approved venue;
(d) if 'Gangsters' is performed as part of a double bill (as with 'Dirty Work' in this case) or together with any other productions in the same venue, the conditions in regard to 'Gangsters' as set out in para 2 shall apply.

The Committee did not impose an age restriction on either play. For obvious reasons, *Gangsters* was considered by the censors to be 'undesirable', but in a context of proclaimed 'reform' by the South African government, the publicity attendant on bannings, detentions and censorship would create an embarrassment for the state. Without banning the play, it was necessary to subject it to some kind of covert control.

The restriction of the play to 'experimental' or 'avant-garde' theatre venues such as The Laager Theatre served, for the Publications Control Board, to anaesthetise the play: with The Market Theatre considered a cultural haven, its function was seen as appropriating political theatre and turning it into a harmless cultural commodity. In the context of the low-level revolutionary action which was at the time prevalent in the townships, theatre in established institutions no longer played the same role in political action. *Gangsters* was as radical a play as has been produced in South Africa, but the state had now to act covertly rather than overtly against political theatre.

In *Jika*, written in 1986, Maponya turns his attention to the difficulties of true political commitment in the struggle for liberation. The play depicts two student leaders who escape death while participating in a political meeting at school. After a period of self-imposed exile in the rural areas of the country they reappear as mature revolutionaries exploring problems of freedom and political activism in the service of the dispossessed people of the country. They attempt to educate dispossessed people about the need for discipline, and for collective communal action: the dispossessed must turn the disadvantages of being landlocked in arid rural areas into advantage through co-operative action and collective social development. Their dream of an ideal political society in which individuals work for the collective good encounters many obstacles as Maponya exposes the contradictions of education, religion, and misguided political action.

Maponya's career is central to a survey of black South African theatre. He is a product of the formative years of Black Consciousness, and also a precursor of the new voice of South African theatre. After decades during which black theatre practitioners and writers had had their voices suppressed or marginalised, by the 1970s these voices had begun to make a profound impact both locally and internationally, primarily because of their congruence with international political pressure against apartheid.

Black theatre practitioners in the 1970s were detained without trial, harassed, and assaulted by the agents of state security, but by the time of the massed people's uprising in June 1976, they had played a prominent role in the movement towards political liberation. It was this political focus that gave black theatre its nationalistic dimension. Although there had been important precursors to the politically-motivated work of theatre practitioners in the 1970s, these had not captured the popular imagination. It was during the 1970s that political consciousness and cultural consciousness found expression in new and innovative forms of performance, and Maponya played a key role in this process.

Ian Steadman
September 1994

SELECT BIBLIOGRAPHY

Anon. *Black Theatre in South Africa*, Fact Paper on South Africa by the International Defence and Aid Fund for Southern Africa, London 1976

T Hauptfleisch & I Steadman, *South African Theatre: Four Plays and an Introduction*, Pretoria: HAUM Press, 1984

T Hauptfleisch and I Steadman (eds), *South African Theatre Journal*, University of Stellenbosch, South Africa.

R Kavanagh, *Theatre and Cultural Struggle in South Africa*, London: Zed Books, 1985

A O'Brien, Staging Whiteness: Beckett, Havel, Maponya, *Theatre Journal 46*, Johns Hopkins University Press, pp 45–61, 1994.

M Orkin, *Drama and the South Africa State*, Witwatersrand University Press, 1992

P Schwartz, *The Best of Company: The Story of Johannesburg's Market Theatre*. Johannesburg: Ad Donker, 1989

I Steadman, Theatre Beyond Apartheid, *Research in African Literatures* (22.3), pp 77–90, 1991

I Steadman, Performance and Politics in Process, *Theatre Survey* (33), pp 188–210, 1992

Derek Goldman

Maishe Maponya, Sydwell Yola and Maile Maponya

THE HUNGRY EARTH

The Hungry Earth was first performed with a cast of five at the Donaldson Orlando Community Centre (DOCC), Soweto in May 1979 and then at the Box Theatre of the University of the Witwatersrand, Johannesburg. With the cast down to three – Maishe Maponya, Dijo Tjabane and Sydwell Yola – it toured Britain professionally from May to August 1981 and then went to Switzerland and West Germany, before returning to its first commercial engagement in South Africa in the Laager at The Market Theatre from January 1982.

This, the complete and final script, was first published in *South Africa Plays* edited by Stephen Gray and published in London by Nick Hern Books and in South Africa by Heinemann-Centaur.

As the house lights fade to blackout, the actors take position and sing:
Wake up Mother Afrika
Wake up
Time has run out
And all opportunity is wasted.
Wake up Mother Afrika
Wake up
Before the white man rapes you.
Wake up Mother Afrika.
As the song ends, the lights come up for:

The Prologue

ALL: We are about to take you on a heroic voyage of the Bahumutsi Drama Group.

ONE: It seems as though some people are without feeling.

TWO: If we would really feel, the pain would be so great that we would stand up and fight to stop all the suffering.

THREE: If we could really feel it in the bowels, the groin, in the throat and in the breast, we would go into the streets and stop the wars, stop slavery, destroy the prisons, stop detentions, stop the killings, stop selfishness – and apartheid we would end.

FOUR: Ah, we would all learn what love is.

FIVE: We would learn what sharing is.

ONE: And, of course, we would live together.

ALL [*singing*]: Touched by our non-violent vibrations.

ONE: We will rise up.

ALL [*singing*]: We will sing while we crawl to the mine.

TWO: We will rise up.

3

ALL [*singing*]:   Bleeding through the days of poverty.

THREE: We will fight hard.

ALL [*singing*]:   Pulsing in the hot dark ground

FOUR: We will rise up.

ALL [*singing*]:   Dying in the stubborn hungry earth. [*Speaking*] We will fight hard.

ALL [*singing*]:
    We will rise up
    And we will sing loud
    Against the hungry earth
    It is our sweat and our blood
    That made Egoli what it is today.

The lights fade, and the actors take up position for:

Scene One: The Hostel

A hostel room. Four men are asleep. One of them is restless. He mumbles and groans and talks incoherently. He tosses about and finally cries out wildly. One of the inmates wakes him. They all wake up.

MATLHOKO (Sufferings): For God's sake, I've been trying to wake you up while you twisted and turned and yelled, 'No, No, No!' like a Salvation Army lass being dragged into a brothel. Do you always have nightmares at dawn?

USIVIKO (Shield): An evil nightmare has been torturing me. My whole body shivers. I wonder if this is real.

BESHWANA (Loincloth): What is it, mngani (friend), tell us quickly.

USIVIKO: I dreamt I saw umlungu (the white man).

SETHOTHO (Imbecile): But we see abelungu (whites) every day of our lives! Why do you behave like a child seeing a ghost when you just dream of umlungu? Don't make dreams your master.

USIVIKO: You are right. This umlungu was far different from them all in a way. This one has divided me against myself. He has tinted my colour. I can no longer distinguish between right and wrong.

BESHWANA: What did this strange umlungu do to you? What did he want?

The lights fade, leaving only MATLHOKO lit.

MATLHOKO: When this land started giving birth to ugly days, things started going wrong from the moment of dawning and peace went into exile, to become a thing of the wilderness. Yes, we experienced the saddest days of our lives when umlungu first came to these shores called Africa, a total stranger from Europe. We received him kindly. We gave him food. We gave him shelter. We adopted his ideas and his teachings. Then he told us of a god and all black faces were full of smiles. When he said love your

5

neighbour we clapped and cheered for we had a natural love. Suddenly we drifted back suspiciously when he said you must always turn the other cheek when you are slapped. He continued to say love those who misuse you. We grumbled inwardly, smiled and listened hard as he was quoting from the Holy Book, little knowing we would end up as puppets on a string, unable to control our own lives. And whilst we were still smiling, he set up laws, organised an army and started digging up the gold and diamonds; and by the time our poor forefathers opened their eyes, umlungu was no more – he had moved to Europe. He has only left his army behind to 'take care of the unruly elements that may provoke a revolution'.

USIVIKO: We will repeat the incident as told by our forefathers.

The lights come up.

MATLHOKO: Men and women of Afrika: umlungu has left us secretly. He has taken with him a great wealth of property, our sheep and cattle, our men and women as servants, gold and silver and all precious stones.

USIVIKO: Let us give chase and get back what he has taken from us. Those riches belong to us, the aborigines of this land.

BESHWANA: Umlungu deserves to die. Let us set out to catch him and when we catch him we will hang him from the nearest tree. His servants must also be killed, they betrayed us. Let us kill the whole lot.

SETHOTHO: You speak of being robbed, you bastards? How can you say such things about umlungu? Before he came you were savages swinging onto trees and eating bananas. You deserted your culture and allowed the hides and wood to rot in the fields. Umlungu taught you how to make leather and how to make furniture. Today you can even make money. You lived like wild animals: now you live like human beings. But no, you ungrateful creatures, you are not satisfied with the things you got from umlungu. Does it surprise you that he has run away?

BESHWANA: How dare you curse my people like that! We blew horns, we beat the drums and we sang the song 'Ngelethu Mawethu' (it is ours, my people), when this land was unknown to the white skins! Shit! We gave culture to the world, we built the pyramids. No! [*pointing a finger at* SETH-OTHO] This man is trying to mislead us! You are obviously a great friend of umlungu. [*Clutching him*] Well, don't worry, we will not separate you from him. You will both be hung from the same tree . . . [*they all lift him above their heads*] and on your combined tombstone we will write:

ALL:

In memory of the oppressor
And his oppressed spy

6

    And to their love-hate
    They were inseparable
In life and in death.
Find no peace.

USIVIKO: We gave chase in thousands. And when we got hold of him his army had received word that we meant to kill umlungu. We first wanted to tell him why we wanted to kill him.

UMLUNGU: What have I done to deserve your enmity? During the two hundred years I dwelt with you I taught you to live a better life. I brought you the wisdom and fertility of Europe. Why is it then that you are after my blood, that you want to kill me and my family?

BESHWANA: You are a stranger, a foreigner. By your labour you merely repaid your debt to our country, your debt to the country that extended its hospitality to you for two hundred years.

UMLUNGU: And why do you want to kill us today? What right have you to look upon yourselves as citizens and upon me as a foreigner?

USIVIKO: You are about to leave this country with all the wealth we sweated our lives for. You underpaid us and celebrated when we were starving. You gave us mirrors and knives in exchange for cattle. You never set foot on those vast tracts of land that are still in their virgin state. You did not want to get to them because you had no slaves to do the sweating for you.

During the next speech and the song the lights fade to half light, and the actors mime the battle of spears against guns.

BESHWANA: We were still arguing when the army attacked from all sides. The spear matched the cowards' weapons from the West and only the crying tone of the singing warrior could be heard.

As the other actors chant softly, BESHWANA *speaks.*

    Stand up all ye brave of Afrika
    Stand up and get to battle,
    Where our brothers die in numbers
    Afrika you are bewitched
    But our black blood will flow
    To water the tree of our freedom.

BESHWANA: Our brave stormed the bullets to protect their motherland from the cruel umlungu. One-two-ten hundreds of our brave never flinched, yet they knew they were heading for death.

Mother Afrika wake up
And arm yourself,
Wipe the tears of your brave
Mother Afrika wake up,
Lest umlungu rapes you
Lest umlungu rapes you

MATLHOKO: Those were ugly days lived by our great-grandfathers, the days of Isandlwana and the days of Umgungundlovu. The days when our forefathers fought hard for what was theirs, for Mother Afrika.

The lights fade to blackout. A song – children singing at work – begins, and the lights come up for:

Scene Two: The Plantation

Three child-workers seated. THE VISITOR, *an investigator, has just entered the* compound.

VISITOR: I am the man who visited Doringkop, owned by Illovo. [*Wandering about, talking to himself*] Ah! so many stables. This man must be very rich to afford so many horses. Let me just peep and see how many horses he has in each. No! This cannot be true. I see people inside. Or maybe they did not look after the cattle well and that's why he locked them inside. Let me just find out. [*He knocks. There is a reply and he goes inside*] Sanibonani.

ALL: Yebo!

VISITOR: I am looking for my son, Sizanani (help one another).

SETHOTHO: USizanani is staying in B Compound. This is A.

VISITOR: Do you all stay in this stable? Why is it that there is no furniture?

ALL: Asazi (We do not know).

VISITOR: How old are you?

MATLHOKO: Mina (Me)?

VISITOR: Yes, wena (you).

MATLHOKO: I am twelve years old and will be thirteen next month.

VISITOR: You? How old are you?

BESHWANA: I am thirteen.

VISITOR: You?

USIVIKO: Twelve.

VISITOR: And you?

MATLHOKO: He is fourteen.

VISITOR: And you?

SETHOTHO: They lie, they are all thirteen years old, I know.

VISITOR: Do you go to school?

BESHWANA: No. We don't go to school. We work for Baas Phuzushugela (Sugardrinker) the whole year.

VISITOR: What does he pay you?

SETHOTHO: He gives me 50c.

BESHWANA: He gives me 70c – I started working last year.

USIVIKO: He gives us all 50c – he is lying. Ubaas Phuzushugela a soze a ku nike i70c (will never give you 70c).

VISITOR: Till when do you work?

BESHWANA: We start at five o'clock in the morning and knock off at three in the afternoon.

VISITOR: When is your lunch?

SETHOTHO: We don't go to lunch. Baas Phuzushugela gives us amageu (sour porridge) and bread at ten o'clock. And once a week we receive rations of mealie meal, beans, salt and meat.

VISITOR: Do you work on Saturdays?

USIVIKO: Yes. Siphumula ngesonto nje (We rest on Sundays).

VISITOR: How far is the sugar field from here?

BESHWANA: Six miles only.

VISITOR: And how do you travel there?

SETHOTHO: We wake up very early and walk.

VISITOR: Tell me, where do you come from?

USIVIKO: We are all from Transkei.

VISITOR: Now how did you come here?

SETHOTHO: Size nge Joini. We are on contract. Will you excuse us, we want to sleep, it is already late.

VISITOR: Where do you sleep?

USIVIKO: Silala lapha (We sleep here).

VISITOR: I immediately went out and eventually ended up in the compound where married men and their wives were staying. Some women told me they earned R1,10 a day and some men said they earned R2 a day after working nine hours. I slept there for a night. I went into the field and was chased because they said I was causing trouble.

10

The child-workers sing.

A SONG OF REJECTION OF TROUBLE-MAKERS
Here comes a man
To cause trouble in my home,
Bring that stick
And I will discipline him . . .

The lights fade as the song ends. The actors move upstage to collect their props, except MATLHOKO *who moves downstage left. Lights up on* MATLHOKO *only, for:* .

Scene Three: The Train

MATLHOKO: Just how I wish I were a spectator of the scenes of the amagoduga (migrant labourers). I would follow them about and just watch every little thing they do and listen to their newly found lingo, Fanagalo. Unfortunately, blacks can never be spectators of white creations, but victims.

Lights full up.

Yes, my wish was misplaced for I was one of the Basotho who were driven by hunger and drought from the confines of their rugged mountains. In those days it seemed as though the god of the white man from over the sea had stamped his feet in anger upon this land for the first time since its creation. Obviously many of us were coming to the mines for the first time. The talk in the crammed compartments was all of the hunger that had fallen in Lesotho. The older men put the blame on the younger generation that had put their faith in the mystical gods of Europe, foolishly forgetting the old and safe ways of the nation's ancestors, and I will never forget what happened on that ugly day in the train . . .

The men, who have been waiting at the station, are now infuriated and angered by the endless waiting. Finally we see four actors occupying chairs which are placed in two parallel rows – the train.

SETHOTHO [*sniffing and looking about and eventually standing to look underneath the seat*]: Hey, man! There is a dangerous odour here. [*Nobody takes notice. He sits down. Then he repeats the same movements.*] Hey, man! I know we all want money but this odour is going to land us in shit!

While he ponders absent mindedly, the compartment door is flung open and a ticket examiner enters, his uniform cap pushed well back from his forehead.

EXAMINER: Kaartjies! Tickets! Come on you black bastards. Hurry up!

12

Standing in the doorway he surveys everybody and wrinkles his nose in disgust. He sniffs the air tentatively three or four times, quickly punches the tickets, and, before leaving, gives them another hard look.

SETHOTHO [*calling out*]: Men of the chief, kere ho a nkga mona (there is a smell here). I can smell matekoane (marijuana). The white man smelled it too. You saw his nose twitching like a jackal's.

BESHWANA [*interrupting*]: O nkgella masepa' mmae fela. Mosima'e towe!

SETHOTHO: I tell you, someone had better throw the matekoane out of the window. At the next station he will inform the police. Will someone please hide the stuff very far lest the police arrest the innocent together with the guilty?

No one moves.

BESHWANA [*imitating the ticket examiner*]: Maak gou (be quick), maak gou, you black skelms!

Laughter.

SETHOTHO [*warning them*]: Hey, my father lived in the City of Gold and he told me there are so many crimes against the law of the white man of which black people might unwittingly be guilty. You will end up in jail if you are found in the streets of the city and can't produce a pass any time and anywhere the police demand it – even in the toilet – I tell you, they sometimes hide in there. If you drink too much you may be arrested for over-indulgence in alcohol. Do you know detention without trial? Section Ten? Or Six? Do you know you can be arrested for being at the wrong place at the wrong time? Do you know house arrest? Do you know Robben Island? Makana? My father knows them all! Pasop banna! [*warningly*] Hlokome-lang! I don't want to repeat my father's experience. Lahlang matekoane ono (Throw it away)!

Realising that his warning is falling on deaf ears, he collects his few belongings to search for another place somewhere in the crowded train. Seeing that he cannot find a place elsewhere, he returns amidst jeers and laughter. They are still laughing when a white sergeant bursts noisily into the compartment with the ticket examiner at his heels. The travellers freeze in sullen silence.

EXAMINER [*eyeing them coldly*]: Come! You black bastards! Where's the dagga? [*No one answers.*] All right! Out onto the platform, you baboons! [*He slaps and kicks the slow ones. Outside, he searches them thoroughly and, finding nothing, he pushes his cap to the very back of his head and turns into the compartment to start his search again. Finally he comes out*

13

swelling like a bullfrog in anger, holding a bag in his hand. He lifts it up and asks:] Wie se sak is hierdie (whose bag is this)?

ALL: We do not know, Sir.

EXAMINER: Go! All into the police vans.

They all end up in the vans, after putting up some resistance during which one is threatened with a bullet in the head. 'Interrogation' and sentencing follow. The lights slowly fade except for the narrator's area downstage right.

USIVIKO: Most of us were 'requested' to produce passes and permits. Those who failed to produce spent two weeks in jail and were deported to their respective homes on their release. This is the inhuman and unjust procedure to endorse the unjust laws that make another a stranger in the land of his birth and rob him of his freedom to move wherever he wants. Is freedom not the law of nature? Then what?

The lights come up for:

Scene Four: The Mine

MATLHOKO [*from the window of his room*]: Hey, Mzala (cousin)!

BESHWANA [*responding through his window*]: Kuyabanda namhlanje, Mzala (It is cold today, cousin).

MATLHOKO: Yes Mzala! The wind . . . It's freezing today.

BESHWANA: The gods are angry.

MATLHOKO: Yes, but their anger can't go beneath this earth. It is quiet there.

A traditional gumboot dance with song. A siren sounds. The lights fade for scene underground. The mineworkers gather at the cage to begin their night shift. The cage descends. It slows to a shuddering halt, and they swarm out like ants to their various places of work. They stoop low, twist and turn to avoid the wooden props which pit their strength against the full weight of the rocky roof that presses down on their crouching heads. Jannie, a white miner, inspects a work face and gives orders.

JANNIE: Tonight I want holes to be drilled here . . . and here . . . and here . . . and here.

BESHWANA [*after a short while*]: Sorry, master, this area may not be suitable, and besides the rock seems wet.

JANNIE: I did not ask your opinion. Do you want to argue with me when I tell you to work?

BESHWANA: I am sorry makhulubaas (big boss), I'm sorry.

They drill at the rock.

BAASBOY [*fuming*]: Hei! Wena! Why tell makhulubaas and not me? Do you want to take my job?

BESHWANA [*apologetic*]: I'm sorry, Baasboy.

BAASBOY: Next time you'll be fired! Pasop, jong (watch out, boy)!

15

JANNIE: Baasboy! Wat gaan aan daarso, jong (What's going on there boy)?

BAASBOY: Makhulubaas, this one thinks he knows too much!

JANNIE: Werk, julle bliksems!

BESHWANA AND BAASBOY: Dankie (Thank you), makhulubaas.

BAASBOY [*pointing a finger at* BESHWANA]: Jy moet werk, jong!

Suddenly there is a great explosion. The miners collapse. Smoke and coughing. Again and again the miners scream in pain and fright.

SETHOTHO: Without even considering the weight of the risk, I stood up, passing the dead bodies of my brothers just to save this sole white skin.

As JANNIE *screams again and again* SETHOTHO *comes to his rescue.*

MATLHOKO: And when the first two ambulances arrived we limped towards them but only makhulubaas was allowed into one. The other turned back because the two ambulances were for the white people only. I looked back into the tunnel where my brothers were being eaten by this hungry earth. I cursed the white man and questioned the very existence of God, for it was my sweat and bones and blood that made Egoli what it is today.

BESHWANA: This is actual fact. Two years after this horrible accident I was transferred to Carletonville where we staged a strike . . .

The actors change positions and start milling around, ignoring the siren that beckons them to work.

BESHWANA [*pointing a finger at* SETHOTHO, *the induna (headman)*]: Wena, induna, you side with the white man today, you must pack your belongings and go to stay with him in the city. We are sick of this induna business!

SETHOTHO [*reassuring them*]: I'm behind you in everything!

COMPOUND MANAGER: Look at these fools! Didn't you hear the machine? [*The miners all keep quiet as he goes to them one by one.*] Hey, wena. Yini wena haikhona sebenza (Hey man, you don't want to work)?

SETHOTHO: Haikhona baas, thina aiyazi sebenzela lo pikinini mali fana ga so (No boss, we can't work for so little money)!

BESHWANA: Baas wena haikhona yipha thina lo insurance, manje thina haikhona sebenza (You refuse to insure us, now we won't work)!

COMPOUND MANAGER: Wena yini ga lo sikhalo ga wena (What is your complaint)?

MATLHOKO: Lo mali wena ga lo yipha thina, thina haikhona satisfied. Kudala lo thina sebenza lapha mgodi. Kodwa wena haikhona yipha lo thina in-

16

crease. Lo room thina hlala, fana ga lo toilet (We are not satisfied with the salary. We have long been working in the mine yet you refuse to give us an increase. The room we stay in is as small as a toilet)!

COMPOUND MANAGER: You! What is your complaint? What? No complaint? Now, all of you, listen to me very carefully because I'm not going to repeat myself! The first thing: you get free lodging. The second thing: you get free food. [*A sudden murmur of discontent.*] The third thing: you get free overalls, free gumboots ...

A wave of angry protest: he pushes them forward to work, they push him back.

COMPOUND MANAGER: Madoda! Skathi nina haikhona hamba sebenza, mina biza lo maphoisa (Men! If you refuse to go to work I'll go and call the police).

ALL [*threatening him with their hats*]: Hamba (Go)! Hamba!

The COMPOUND MANAGER *can be heard from his office talking to the police.*

COMPOUND MANAGER: Yes sir, anything may happen – they are about to destroy everything, they are wild, come quickly!

ALL: The police won, but not without declaring themselves enemies of the people!

COMPOUND MANAGER: We shall not be intimidated.

There is the sound of a machine-gun and as some miners fall down, some raise their hands, surrendering to go down into the mine. MATLHOKO *continues relating what happened.*

MATLHOKO: Yes, we were forced to go down in Carletonville though we knew that this earth was hungry. Who would listen to our cries? Yes, never will I forget that bloody Sharpeville for I was there in 1960 when an anti-pass campaign was opened.

They produce passes and interact with each other as they express their anger and disgust at the pass system. BESHWANA *throws his pass away, but is advised not to do so.*

USIVIKO: Hei Beshwana, not here! At the police station. Come, everybody, let us go to the police station.

BESHWANA: Let us throw stones then. We must put up a fight.

They stop him from throwing stones.

USIVIKO: You are giving them a wrong impression of us. We are not violent people. And this is a peaceful demonstration. Come everybody ...

A procession and the burning of passbooks, with a song.

Senze ntoni na?	What have we done?
Senze ntoni na?	
Nkosi mthetheleli	God, our spokesman
Si bhekisa kuwe	We put all our faith in You
Yini na? Ukuba sibenjana?	Why have we to live this way
Sikhulule kuwo lamatyatanga	Release us from these shackles.
Sikhulule kuwo lamatyatanga	
Senze ntoni na?	
Senze ntoni na?	

As they put their passes on the fire, the lights fade until only the fire remains. The song continues.

USIVIKO: The police panicked at the sight of the massed though unarmed innocent black faces . . .

ALL: We were all of the same frame of mind . . .

USIVIKO: And they opened fire! [*Mimes firing at the protestors as they fall to the ground.*] I went to the funeral and was shocked to see how hungry this earth is, for it had opened to swallow the black man. Those who survived were arrested and charged with incitement to violence under the Public Safety Act . . . someone somewhere did not understand 'peaceful' and 'violent'. . . Anyhow, let's forget about that because some very rich white women and some elite black women have formed 'Women for Peace' and I hope they will forget their elitism and their socialising process and be equally dedicated to peace in Afrika.

Saluting with a clenched fist, he stretches and flexes his body like a person who's just woken up from a sleep.

Scene Five: The Compound

Sunday morning activity inside a compound room.

BESHWANA [*waking up from a sleep and calling out to* USIVIKO]: We mgani wami. Come here . . . I went to the biggest shebeen in the township yesterday.

USIVIKO: Kuphi lapho (Where's that)?

BESHWANA: At Rose's place.

USIVIKO: Rose's shebeen?

BESHWANA: Ngathenga ugologo mngani wami . . . ngathi laca . . . laca . . . laca . . . (I bought liquor and had so much to drink).

USIVIKO: You must have been drunk.

BESHWANA: Yebo mngani wami . . . ngase ngi lala la – here on the floor.

USIVIKO: So you slept here, hey! That's not good for your health. You must stop drinking . . . And who was burning papers on the floor?

BESHWANA: Where?

USIVIKO: Behind you.

BESHWANA: I don't know.

USIVIKO: You will know when this place goes up in flames . . . ga!

BESHWANA [*angered*]: I said I don't know . . .

USIVIKO: Okay! You don't have to shout at me!

BESHWANA: Fuck off!

USIVIKO: You must count your words when you talk to me. Ga!

BESHWANA [*emphasising each word*]: Go to hell!

USIVIKO [*as he removes the ash, frustrated*]: Okay! I will meet you there!

There is tension between the two. Silence.

19

BESHWANA [*a little later*]:   Hey, my friend! Did you hear the latest news? [*Silence.*] The manager has requested us to do the traditional dance for the tourists.

USIVIKO: When will we ever have a Sunday of our own? You're used to dancing every Sunday. Are you going to do it again today in that drunk state?

BESHWANA: No, I've grown old, Sonnyboy. I can't dance anymore . . . [*Silence*] Hey, can you see out there?

USIVIKO: What?

BESHWANA: The bus, my friend . . . [*He looks out of the window.*] Can you see it . . . there!

USIVIKO: Look . . . SAR Tours. It's the tourists. Look, they've got cameras aimed at us. They are taking a picture of us.

They pose for a picture. They are in a happy mood as they run out of the room.

BESHWANA: There it stops, my friend. They've got tape recorders . . . [*They walk towards the dance area.*] Hey, another picture . . .

They hug and pose.

ALL: Hi! Hello, beautiful tourists . . . Welcome to sunny South Africa! Hello . . .

BESHWANA: Another picture. [*Pose.*] They're taking their seats. Come closer. [*Talks softly to him.*] Can you see that man over there?

USIVIKO: Which one?

BESHWANA: The one with small eyes . . . He looks like eh . . .

USIVIKO: He looks like . . . Mao Tse Tung.

BESHWANA: But I'm scared, my friend. Can you see the two men beside him? They look like the Security Branch.

USIVIKO: Oh, pity he's escorted.

BESHWANA [*sudden excitement*]:   My friend, my friend, look . . .

USIVIKO: I see . . .

BESHWANA: That bearded one . . . what do you think?

USIVIKO: Yeh! He looks like Karl Marx!

They seem to have fun with their explorations. They point at a lady in the arena whom they agree looks 'like Lady Diana!' Finally . . .

BESHWANA: Can you see that black man sitting alone there? He looks like . . .

USIVIKO: Shame . . . that one, simple . . .

20

BOTH: He is the bus driver! Ha ha ha!

They call out to MATLHOKO, *whom they've nicknamed Manikiniki.*

BOTH: We Manikiniki! Manikiniki!

BESHWANA: Come out!

USIVIKO: The tourists are here!

MATLHOKO: What? Just leave me alone.

BESHWANA: Come out! Come and see for yourself. Tourists!

MATLHOKO: Terrorists?

USIVIKO: No, tourists!

MATLHOKO *comes out dressed in traditional garb and finally they dance and entertain the tourists, drumming and singing and posing for pictures until they are exhausted.*

Scene Six: The Compound

Everyday activity. A gramophone plays a Zulu tune, gambling, cooking, finally fighting.

MATLHOKO: Heje, I read a true statement in the Bible last week: it says we shall live by the sweat of our brows.

SETHOTHO: Oh, how true that is, mngani – it's amazing. [*Starts coughing.*] But it's time I go on pension. I'm old and my chest seems to be dry or maybe I have run out of blood. I'm scared.

MATLHOKO: Ja we must; you remember when we started here way back in the fifties. We were still young boys. Then you could hardly speak Sesotho, only Xhosa. Of course I did not trust you. Yooo! who could trust a Xhosa lad anyway? [*They laugh.*] You remember we thought we would work ouselves up, bring our families down here and buy a 'Buick master road'. But here we are now, still struggling and about to die, no Buick and wives still far away.

SETHOTHO: Hey, you remind me of the houses outside the perimeter of this compound. Hey man, the scene is pathetic . . . there are women there!

MATLHOKO: What are you talking about?

SETHOTHO: I mean, have you not seen those rusted, corrugated iron huts mixed with pieces of wood and petrol drums?

MATLHOKO: J-jaa, I saw them.

SETHOTHO: Did you know people stay there?

MATLHOKO: Yes, I went there several times. In fact let's get down there now, I feel thirsty.

The lights fade as they exit singing.

WOMAN: My name is Chirango. This is my only home. I came here some five years after my husband had written to me to come and join him in this city of gold. To my dismay, I was not permitted to stay with him. I could not go back to Rhodesia because I had no money. He took me into his room at night. Later when a wall was erected around the compound it became risky to sneak in. Once I was arrested and fined R90 or 90 days. He did not have the money and I went to jail. When I came back I was told that his contract had expired and since then I have never seen or heard of him. Today I manage to live and feed my two fatherless children out of the beers and indambola (liquor) I sell. And when the beers don't sell I become every man's woman. What else can I do? I can't get permits to work here.

THE WOMAN'S SONG
I'll never get to Malawi
I'll never get to Transkei
I'll never get to Bophuthatswana

The lights come up as men enter, singing. They tease her, eventually settling down.

MATLHOKO: Sisi, is Chirango your name or your husband's?

WOMAN: It is my husband's. Why?

SETHOTHO: Yes, I thought as much. Your name rings a bell. I worked with a Chirango some two years ago in the Western Transvaal gold mine near Orkney. He was tall, dark, hefty – and wore a moustache ...

WOMAN: Where is he? He is the father of my children! He is my husband! I want him.

SETHOTHO: This is a very sorry state of affairs. I even fear to talk about it.

WOMAN [*anxious*]: Tell me! Where is my husband?

SETHOTHO [*relating in a rather pathetic tone*]: Your husband was among the forty-one black miners trapped underground in a raging fire who were left to die when mine authorities gave the order to seal off the passageways. I was among the 233 mine workers who were affected by the fumes and were treated in hospital.

WOMAN [*hysterical and crying*]: Oh, how cruel this earth is. Our men will never stop dying to feed this hungry earth. Today I have no place to stay. Today I am a widow. Today my children are fatherless yet I do not know. How many more have vanished like that without the knowledge of immediate relatives? My husband has died digging endlessly for gold which would help to prop up the apartheid system. My man is dead! My man is eaten by the hungry earth! He is dead!

23

The lights fade slowly. Group song.

S'thandwa s'thandwa
S'thandwa se nhliziyo yam
(Beloved one of my heart)
Beloved one, dry your tears
Daughter of Afrika
Somandla! Somandla!
Uphi na Qamatha?
(Almighty! Where art thou?)
When this hungry earth
Swallows, swallows
Thy children
Somandla! Somandla!
Sikelela Insapho, ye Afrika
Nkosi Sikelela thina lusapholwayo
(Bless the family of Afrika)
Sikelela insapho, ye Afrika
Nkosi Sikelela thina lusapholwayo.

EPILOGUE SONG
Where have all our men gone
They have all gone down into the mines
They will never return again
They have been swallowed up by this hungry earth!

Lights fade to blackout.

Maile Maponya

Back: Maishe Maponya, Bennette Tlouana
Front: Gcina Mhlophe, Fumane Kokome

UMONGIKAZI/THE NURSE

Umongikazi was first performed at the Donaldson Orlando Community Centre Soweto, in 1983 and featured Gcina Mhlophe, Fumane Kokome, Bennette Tlouana and Maishe Maponya. It later opened at The Market Theatre for three weeks and, immediately thereafter, played to packed houses at Glynn Thomas (Baragwanath Hospital) with the same cast. At the end of the third performance at Glynn Thomas, the writer was ordered to go to Protea Police Station for 'a friendly chat' (sic). There he was interrogated by the Security Police.

The play later toured Germany, Switzerland and the United Kingdom, originally without the two leading performers, Gcina Mhlophe and Maishe Maponya who were refused passports, 'for security reasons'.

Later performances in South Africa featured Thoko Ntshinga, Nomhle Tokwe, Oupa Mthimkulu and Maishe Maponya

Cast

FEZILE... early thirties.

NYAMEZO... A nurse. Twenty-eight years old. Fezile's wife.

MARIA... A nurse. In her mid-thirties.

ACTOR FOUR... Portrays several characters indicated in the text.

MAHLALELA, DR LUMUMBA, BLACK DOCTOR, MALE NURSE, LOCAL SE-CURITY are played by the actor who plays FEZILE.

PAEDIATRICIAN, PATIENTS (Sc 6), FIRST NURSE (Sc 6), SECOND NURSE (Sc 6); THIRD NURSE (Sc 6) are played by the actress who plays NYAMEZO.

OLD WOMAN, NURSE (Sc 1), NURSE (Sc 4), MATRON, THEATRE MATRON, NURSE (Sc 5), MAGOGO, THIRD NURSE (Sc 7) are played by the actress who plays MARIA.

WHITE DOCTOR, DR OWEN, PREGNANT WOMAN, QUEUE MARSHALL, PHARMACIST, SECOND MALE NURSE, POLICE OFFICIAL are portrayed by ACTOR FOUR.

SETTING: Stage right takes only a third of the stage and serves as FEZILE's home. It is sometimes used as an exit area from stage left. Stage left takes two-thirds of the whole stage as the Hospital. When action moves from one stage to the other the Transition is indicated by a lighting change. Some scenes and episodes are flashbacks; these all take place in the Hospital.

PROPS AND COSTUMES: Two garden chairs and a small round table for stage right. A normal size table and a chair for stage left. A typical hospital screen, four chairs.

Nurses' white uniforms, Matron's uniform, theatre overalls and caps, khaki watchman's uniform and a knobkierrie, blue man's overall, hedge-cutter, shirt, white shoes, doctors' uniforms and overcoat, stethoscope, surgical scissors, incubator, four pairs of spectacles (different kinds), two brown wigs, one Afro wig, newspapers (*Nursing News*), a normal sized yo-yo and an extra large yo-yo (the size of a vehicle tyre), a brown file, small board with the word 'Chemist' on it and two sticks at the edges to hold it, telephone, two white masks (different kinds), a hair brush, bucket containing water, soap, a washing rag, a walking stick, floral dress and a cap (for old woman), hospital pyjamas.

Scene One

Blackout. Spotlight comes up on an OLD WOMAN *singing an overture; a background to the struggle. The song is entitled 'Ntsikana' and is sung in Xhosa.*

OLD WOMAN:

Wayetshilo uNtsikana	Ntsikana said
Wayetshilo umfo kaGabha	The son of Gabha said
Ukuth' umzomnyama uyophalala	That the black home will be spilled
Ngenene waphalala njengamanzi	And truly it was spilled like water
Wayetshilo wathi nothengisana	He had said that you will sell each other
Nithegisane	Sell each other for the button without holes (money)
ngeqosh'elingenamxunya	
Amadoda ahlele ezinjwaleni	Men are now in the drinking place
Abafazi base marabini	The women are lost to marabi
Kwenze njani na mzikaPhalo	What's wrong home of Phalo?
Wovuswa ngubani xa ulelenje	Who'll wake you up as you sleep?
Ahambile 'amaqhawe amahle	The beautiful heroes have gone
Ahambile ngenxa yo mzomnyama	They have gone for the sake of the black home
Abanye bakufele wena Afrika	Others have died for you Afrika
'Banye base mazweni	Others are prisoners in foreign lands.
bangamabanjwa'	
Uzovuka nini	When will you wake up?
Uzovuka nini we Afrika	When will you wake up Afrika?
Zayaphin' inkokheli	Where have the leadership of the black home gone?
zomzomnyama	
Ndihlab'umkhosi	I am making a call
Ndihlab'umkhosi ndithi vukani kusile	I am making a call to say wake up it's dawn

Vukani kusile magwala ndini	Wake up it's dawn you cowards
Ndiyalila ndilel' umzomnyama	I mourn the black home
Ndithi ziphi inkokhelizawo	Where is its leadership?
Hlobanizikhali iyohlasela	Arm yourself and attack
Vukani kusile magwala ndini!	Wake up it's dawn you cowards!

The lights come up slowly stage left on the PATIENTS *at the rear. The* DOCTOR *is visiting the patients in the ward. He goes from one bed to the other with* SISTER NYAMEZO *assisting in translations and other regular duties.* SISTER NYAMEZO *is delayed at the back talking to a patient.*

DOCTOR [*calling to* NYAMEZO]: Sister Nyamezo please come and help here.

NYAMEZO: I'm coming Doctor . . . [*She follows him.*]

DOCTOR: . . . And who is this one?

NYAMEZO: Mandla, doctor.

DOCTOR: I see . . . Breath in Mandla . . . Again . . . Okay. Open your mouth wider, . . . say ahhh! Ahhh! [*Examines him. Turns to* NYAMEZO.] I think he's all right.

DOCTOR [*as they move away from the patients*]: Good, sister . . . I am satisfied with the progress of all the patients. As you heard, I may discharge about three of them tomorrow if their condition stays good. But, there is one patient I haven't seen in a long time . . . what on earth is happening to him?

NYAMEZO: Mahlalela doctor?

DOCTOR: That's right sister.

NYAMEZO: He's always here at night. The sister I relieved this morning tells me he sleeps all night, but as soon as she knocks off and I take over, he disappears. He was given his medication last night . . . here, look at his report . . .

DOCTOR: Remember sister, the patients are your sole responsibility. I want to see that patient tomorrow. Just imagine, I've had this ward for the past three weeks, yet I haven't seen all my patients. Make sure that I see Mahl-Mahl . . . NYAMEZO: Mahlalela doctor . . .

DOCTOR: Never mind about the name, sister . . . I want to see him! [*He rushes out.*]

Scene Two

Early the next morning. NYAMEZO *bursts into the hospital ward only to bump into* MAHLALELA *who is preparing to sneak out.* MAHLALELA *is dressed in hospital pyjamas, he has his personal clothes in his hands.*

NYAMEZO: Ja, and where are you off to?

MAHLALELA: To the toilet, sister – out of my way I'm pressed, I'm in a hurry . . . Nurse khaundiyeke torho (just leave me alone please)!

He tries to push past.

Enter on-duty NURSE.

NURSE: What on earth is happening here? What's wrong sister? Why are you so early today?

NYAMEZO: I want to see a certain patient. I miss him every day because as soon as you knock off he disappears. The doctor wants to know what he is up to . . .

NURSE: Which patient is that?

NYAMEZO: Mahlalela.

NURSE: Mos nank'uMahlalela (But here is Mahlalela).

MAHLALELA: Leave me alone women, you are wasting your time, I want to go . . .

NURSES: Where to?

MAHLALELA: Toilet! . . . Since when do you stop patients from going to the toilet? Watch out . . . I'll report you to the doctor!

NURSE: But the toilet is at the other end Mahlalela!

MAHLALELA [*louder*]: I want to take some fresh air before I go to the toilet.

NURSE [*angry*]: That's madness! What air? Go straight to the toilet or go back to sleep!

32

MAHLALELA: No one is going to tell me what to do. I do what I like here, I warn you women, get out of my way!

NYAMEZO: Remember you are a patient here and we are in charge of all patients. We tell the patients what to do.

MAHLALELA: Not me!

NURSE: You included!

MAHLALELA: If I lose my job because of late coming you will lose yours the next day. Get out of my way I'm late. [*He pushes them aside.*] I am going to work . . .

NYAMEZO: He is mad! We must report him to the Superintendent.

NURSE: No sister, it is dangerous.

NYAMEZO [*puzzled*]: Why?

NURSE: Mahlalela stayed on in hospital after he was discharged, that was three weeks ago. And every morning when he wakes up he goes straight to work . . .

CHORUS OF PATIENTS: Fifteen thousand people have been on the waiting list for fifteen years. No houses! Where do you expect him to live?

Exit all except NURSE.

NURSE [*laughs as she recalls*]: And . . . I know of a certain patient who apparently had an agreement with the doctor. This one was never discharged from the hospital because he had to clean the doctor's car every morning!

Exit NURSE *laughing.*

Scene Three

FEZILE's home. Enter NYAMEZO *still dressed in her white hospital uniform – from work. On the small garden table are several copies of* Nursing News. *Her attention is drawn to the headline on the first paper which she reads aloud.*

NYAMEZO: 'Be positive, despite problems' [*She throws it away, sits down, and takes a look at another.*] 'Call on SANA members. Before you raise your voice to criticise the South African Nursing Association along with other uninformed people, make the effort to find out what the association does for its members, particularly in the area of salaries' [*She looks disappointedly at yet another.*] 'A Christmas message from our President'. Very interesting [*Stands up to read it carefully.*] 'As the year draws to a close, my thoughts go out to all the nurses of South Africa who, in this exceptionally difficult year have served the nation with dignity, devotion and distinction. Have faith in your future – a better deal for nurses is just around the corner.' Shit!

Enter FEZILE *in a happy mood.*

FEZILE [*with both hands clutched together, hiding something. He sings*]: I've got the world in my hands ... I've got the world at my fingertips ...

NYAMEZO: And what is that supposed to mean?

FEZILE: It's a song ...

NYAMEZO: I know that, but what are you doing?

FEZILE: The conquest of nature by Fezile – a discovery. I am yo-yoing ... [*He parts his hands to reveal a long string with a yo-yo at the end.*] First I yo, and then yo again ... Thus producing a familiar repetitive motion known as yo-yoing ... One of these days my name will go down in the history books of the world. How would you feel about it? Obviously great!

34

And what is that supposed to mean? [*He gestures at the papers with his head.*]

NYAMEZO: What?

FEZILE: Papers on the floor!

NYAMEZO: Rubbish! Rubbish! I can't stand reading these papers these days. I often wonder why we have to pay subscription fees each year. It is as if the black nurse does not exist. Nothing is said about us and the progress we make.

FEZILE [*ignoring her*]: Well I'm conquering gravity, proving that what goes down must come up.

NYAMEZO: Will you stop that and start clearing this mess, if you don't want to listen – go and trim the hedge!

FEZILE [*continues with his yo-yo tricks*]: I thought as much – look, look I told you. I'm conquering nature! [*Sings*] I've got the world spinning and spinning at my command . . .

NYAMEZO: You are wasting time! Will you clear up this mess?

FEZILE: I'll clear it up when I've done this my dear.

NYAMEZO: I know you won't.

FEZILE: I will. Look at that skill! Makes me feel like a god. A movement of my hand and the world spins my way. [*Sings*] Give it a twist, just a flick of the wrist.

NYAMEZO [*peering at something she missed as she went through the papers and pulling the whole page out*]: Yes, this is where it all began, the whole story of the nursing council – all in one phrase . . .

FEZILE: Shoo! Ain't funny? Keeps on going down and up again – I can't stop it . . .

NYAMEZO: I sometimes think you don't live in the same world as the rest of us. The only thing you are concerned about is that daft toy. Does nothing get through to you? Does your mind drift through your head like foggy smoke with no direction, no purpose?

FEZILE *continues to yo-yo.*

FEZILE: You should relax my darling . . .

NYAMEZO [*irritated*]: You don't understand, just put that thing away.

FEZILE: It is a cord. An umbilical cord between me and peace . . .

NYAMEZO: Some shit cord!

FEZILE: Well it keeps me alive.

NYAMEZO *walks out angrily. She comes back with a pair of hedge-cutters and in a split second cuts the string of the yo-yo leaving* FEZILE *with his mouth open in disbelief. Silence.*

NYAMEZO: With that out of the way you will probably listen to me!

FEZILE: Damn it! I have no spare string . . .

NYAMEZO: Thank God for that.

FEZILE: I shall mend it. Though it will never be the same again because the knot will make it jerk . . .

NYAMEZO: At least you will now have to listen to me!

FEZILE [*getting a new idea*]: Wait a minute. I am going to devise a new trick. This time I won't have to use the string. And you know what? Some mad-caps around the world will be identifying it as an unidentified flying object . . . I'm going to do it I'm telling you . . . [*He tries to leave*]

NYAMEZO: All I'm telling you now is to go and trim the hedge! What kind of husband are you? It's toys, toys . . . an old man like you. You should be ashamed of yourself!

FEZILE *picks up the cutters and reluctantly starts to trim the hedge.* NYAMEZO *picks up another* Nursing Times *and begins to read.*

NYAMEZO: Fezile! Fezile! Do you know that Dr Lumumba has resigned?

FEZILE: What?

NYAMEZO: Yes, he is leaving at the end of this month. Apparently he is leaving the country too.

FEZILE: Rubbish! I can't believe it.

NYAMEZO: 'Rubbish! I can't believe it.' It's here in this useless paper. I understand his reasons though . . . how can they expect him to drive all the way from Benoni to Attridgeville in that old skodonk every day, that's wrong! They should give him transport allowance. Not only that . . .

Flashback.

Enter a white DOCTOR *giving information to trainees.*

DOCTOR: Look, working in this place you've got all the advantages on earth. A good salary – a really good salary – you attend to only a few patients like of course in the white hospitals. Granted there is congestion everywhere in the black hospitals, but you have all those sisters who have done primary health care to assist you. They are always around. You will get travelling allowance no matter where you come from. We don't expect you to come all the way from Cape Town for work. And another advantage is that you are a white-doctor-in-a-black hospital . . . Ever thought of that? Yes, tolerance fee! I presume that we are serving a different community group . . . that is our compensation . . . Tolerance fee!

End of flashback

NYAMEZO: Yes but these are precisely the reasons for his resignation. You see, apartheid is rooted in the hospitals too. Dr Lumumba was the first to realise this and he made us aware of it. Oh how I'm going to miss those moments when Dr Lumumba would call us like a father to his children.

Exit FEZILE. NYAMEZO *moves to stage left.*

Flashback. Enter FEZILE *as* DR LUMUMBA.

DR LUMUMBA [*calling out to* NYAMEZO]: Sister! Sister! Nyamezo!

NYAMEZO: Yes doctor.

DR LUMUMBA: Listen. Whether you accept it or not, the truth is right in front of you. Whilst we appreciate the progress you as nurses are making, we are not blind to the fact that this move is not only to alleviate the pressure in the clinics. No! It's also an economic strategy by the Department of Health. None of us is getting what the white doctor's get and we examine the patients just as well as they do.

NYAMEZO: But Dr Lumumba, it's an opportunity we have to grab. At the end of it we'll know what every doctor knows . . .

DR LUMUMBA [*raising his voice*]: That doesn't make you a doctor. Why train a lot of health workers instead of educating people? It's ridiculous – out of 23 million black people how many qualified black doctors have we got in the country – less than 4 000? And out of five million whites how many qualified white doctors are there? More than 12 000! The education system is rotten! And once you've come to this conclusion, you must start suspecting the teacher, suspect the book he reads from, suspect the school principal, the regional inspector and the whole bloody education system!

NYAMEZO [*shocked*]: Dr Lumumba!

Exits to reappear stage right.

DR LUMUMBA [*softer and slower*]: Yes, frustration of the black mother frustrates the black child and the result is a social breakdown of black life – that's why we have what they call in our schools 'drop-outs'!

Exit DR LUMUMBA.

End of flashback.

NYAMEZO: That was the man – Dr Lumumba. To think that he is no longer with us . . . He used to smart every nurse's ear with wisdom. He would say this in front of everyone. He would even say it to the officials . . .

FEZILE [*still backstage*]: Hai! hai! hai! Would he have said it in the presence of whites?

NYAMEZO: What whites? Aren't whites officials? Oh how we used to admire his convictions. And now to think that he's gone. What a loss!

FEZILE *comes out with a bucket full of water and soap all over his head and face.*

FEZILE: Now I see Dr Lumumba has chosen a wrong profession.

NYAMEZO: That is the man who has given me the right education . . .

FEZILE: Wrong education. That man is not supposed to be a doctor.

NYAMEZO: His education was spiritually uplifting . . .

FEZILE: Wrong education . . .

NYAMEZO: Right education!

FEZILE: I'm telling you that kind of education is wrong . . .

NYAMEZO: That's the right education!

Enter MARIA *as they continue to scream at each other.*

Scene Four

MARIA: Hi Nyamezo! Hi Fezile!

NYAMEZO & FEZILE [*surprised*]: Hi Maria, hi!

NYAMEZO: Long time no see Maria. Where have you been, what's up?

MARIA: Nyamezo, I am the most disillusioned nurse in the country. Things are bad for me, I'm out of work again.

NYAMEZO: Come now Maria, we are busy discussing something serious about Dr Lumumba and here you come with one of your silly jokes.

MARIA: Serious, I've lost my job.

FEZILE: Come on Maria, not so long ago you were telling us how nice it was to be working in the white hospitals . . . and so what's gone wrong?

MARIA: Yes Fezi, but remember greener pastures are always full of snakes, poisonous snakes! The other nurses have not resigned but it's going to become very difficult for them there. Nowadays, the black nurses are put at the mercy of people we never thought mattered a lot in the hospitals.

NYAMEZO: Like?

MARIA: Like the white cooks of course. [NYAMEZO *and* FEZILE *burst out laughing.*] Just imagine a fat white woman who has no inkling of what it is like to be a nurse, exercising her unprofessional status on a black qualified nurse. [*She enacts the scenario.*] 'I will fire you! I will fire you my girl! If you don't know how to behave in front of your seniors, this is not the place to learn that! I'm your senior and I will bloody fire you!'

NYAMEZO [*laughing*]: Is that what happens?

MARIA: For God's sake! To think she's got an apron and I've got epaulettes and bars to show status, but to her status is this. [*She points to her cheeks.*] The thing that makes me mad is that we are barred from attending to some

39

patients because there is a general complaint from the patients that they don't feel safe when they are attended to by black nurses . . .

FEZILE: Ja Maria, to expect to work harmoniously with the white nurses is impossible. It won't work. Just won't work! You see we come from different places, different homes and different cultures. Apartheid has damaged the minds of the white people. The only thing that puts them together is the iron hand!

NYAMEZO: Exactly!

MARIA: To rub salt into the wound, black nurses at Wenela hospital are now being instructed to leave their uniforms behind when they knock off.

NYAMEZO: Why, so they are not seen to be working there?

MARIA: Precisely. You know in white hospitals we are treated like assistant nurses. When the white nurses are scrubbing . . .

FEZILE: Come on Maria, do you want to tell us that white nurses scrub floors too? No we can't believe this one.

MARIA: No Fezi . . . I don't mean that. What I mean is that when they are in the middle of an operation . . .

FEZILE: Oh I see, that's hospital terminology . . .

MARIA: Yes Fezi. This is not a layman's language. What I mean is that when they are in the middle of an operation, I have to wait on the sidelines and take instructions from them . . . And the other thing that really made me mad was when I discovered their 'skinder-hoekie' (gossip corner)!

NYAMEZO: A what?

MARIA: Yes a skinder-hoekie. You know, they keep a 'skinderboek' (gossip log).

FEZILE: Maria tell us why they call it a 'skinderboek'. What a name!

MARIA: Because that's where they sharpen their scalpels!

FEZILE [shocked]: Scalpels. Shoo! That's a dangerous weapon. Hai, white people in this country are a disaster to black people.

He exits with the bucket and comes back with a hair brush.

MARIA: Sister Nyamezo, I think I am going to rejoin the black hospitals. I will learn to tolerate the attitudes of other black nurses and black patients, after all they are my people and I understand them.

NYAMEZO: It's high time you did.

MARIA: I think I have to go now. Bye!

Exit MARIA. FEZILE *continues to brush his hair whilst looking himself up and down in the mirror.*

NYAMEZO: Poor Maria . . . To think she was so excited when she was going to this white hospital of hers. And now she's back. Just imagine the white cook . . .

FEZILE: All right, all right, let's forget about Maria for the time being . . .

NYAMEZO: Yes.

FEZILE: I've some business to talk to you about.

NYAMEZO: Some business? Aren't we getting serious these days . . .

FEZILE: Yes we are getting serious.

NYAMEZO: Come, tell me what's the business about?

FEZILE [*quickly*]: Remember the project I told you about?

NYAMEZO: A project? I can't remember talking to you about a project.

FEZILE: Damn it, can't you remember the other day when you asked me to trim the hedge?

NYAMEZO: Yes I remember asking you to trim the hedge.

FEZILE: Ja, that very same day I told you about the project.

NYAMEZO: What kind of project is that? In fact I can't even imagine you involved in a project.

FEZILE: Well you had better start imagining it now.

NYAMEZO: All right tell me, what kind of project is it?

FEZILE [*getting irritated*]: It's a project!

NYAMEZO: Ja, I know it's a project but what kind of project is it?

FEZILE: I need some cash.

NYAMEZO: What for?

FEZILE: For the project.

NYAMEZO: I know but what is the project?

FEZILE: I need to buy some machinery. Actually I want to buy a fuel injection carburettor. Do you know what that is . . . ?

NYAMEZO: Fuel injection carburettor, what a beautiful name for a project . . . but you still haven't told me what the project is. Isn't it boring for me to keep asking what is the project, what is the project, and still I can't get an answer?

FEZILE [*doubtfully*]: Well . . . you know that I am inventing a new . . . Hmm . . . yo-yo.

NYAMEZO: What? A yo-yo. Do you seriously mean you expect me to give you money for a yo-yo? A toy? That'll be the day! Andi soze (I won't)!

She walks out of the house.

FEZILE [*angrily*]: Hei wena mfazi (Hey, woman), give me some money! If you don't want to give me the money bring back my whole pay packet I gave you last Friday – I want my money!

He follows her.

Scene Five

In the casualty theatre where minor cases like circumcision, skin graft or tooth extraction are treated. There is a screen and a FLOOR NURSE *peeps through it.*

NURSE [*to the audience*]:   We were only left with five minutes to finish the case.

Enter DR OWEN. *The* FLOOR NURSE *comes from behind the screen with some instruments. She bumps into* DR OWEN. *The instruments fall to the floor.* DR OWEN *instructs her to pick them up.*

DR OWEN [*puzzled*]:   And now, what's going on in my theatre?

NURSE: We are busy on a case doctor.

DR OWEN: I want an answer from the surgeon.

NURSE: That won't help. All cases must be booked.

DR OWEN [*angrily*]:   But I always get preference you small banana!

NURSE [*fuming*]:   Not this time you big orange!

DR OWEN: You don't call me a big orange, you stupid!

NYAMEZO [*peeping from behind the screen and interrupting*]:   And I never realised there were oranges and bananas working here!

NURSE: Neither did I. I've been trying to tell Doctor Owen that we are busy on a case!

NYAMEZO: And how does he react to that?

NURSE: You know this silly doctor has a bad tendency to bully us around here in the theatre. He even goes to the extent of beating up the patients. He is really getting on my nerves . . .

DR OWEN [*pulls out a gun*]:   I'll shoot you!!

43

NYAMEZO [*bravely*]: That'll be the day.

DR OWEN: I'll shoot you too!

NURSE: Do it now . . .

Exit OWEN *to call the* MATRON.

NYAMEZO [*agitated*]: A doctor pointing a gun at us! I'm going to report this matter to the nursing council!

The NURSE *rushes out. She returns as the* MATRON, *closely followed by* DR OWEN, *to confront* NYAMEZO.

MATRON [*not even waiting to hear the other side of the story*]: Sister! It's indecent to talk so arrogantly to the doctor. Remember that he has sacrificed years of his life for this hospital . . .

NYAMEZO: If you talk to me in that attitude I will not waste my breath!

DR OWEN: Hear, I told you. This is the kind of people the hospitals employ these days, cheeky! I will report this matter to the chief matron! You are not solving my problem either!

He pulls the MATRON *by the hand.*

MATRON: Don't pull me so hard doctor!

The MATRON *exits and returns as* THEATRE MATRON. *She has hardly opened her mouth to speak when* DR OWEN *starts.*

DR OWEN [*still angry*]: These little bananas have a tendency to call me names!

NYAMEZO: There he goes again calling us . . .

DR OWEN: Shut up!

T MATRON [*questioning* NYAMEZO]: Sister, where were you in nineteen seventy-six?

NYAMEZO: Don't crack your skull. I had already begun working here!

T MATRON: Well, here we don't behave like the nineteen seventy-six children!

DR OWEN: Bloody terrorists!

T MATRON: And remember sister . . . I am going to write a report about your unprofessional behaviour . . . I'm going to do it!

DR OWEN: I like your attitude matron . . . these nurses need discipline.

T MATRON: Thank you doctor . . .

Exit DR OWEN *and* THEATRE MATRON.

Scene Six

FEZILE's *home. Once more he is seen with a yo-yo in his hands. He seems quite happy with life while something is seriously bothering* NYAMEZO.

FEZILE: Lovie wee!

NYAMEZO: Hee-

FEZILE: I have trimmed the hedge . . .

NYAMEZO: Ja I saw that . . .

FEZILE: And did you see where I planted the lilac bushes? It makes the view better, doesn't it? Lovie, you know what?

NYAMEZO: Ja . . .

FEZILE: You don't look too good today.

NYAMEZO: I know.

FEZILE: But you didn't tell me why?

NYAMEZO: How can I talk sense to you when that daft toy still occupies your mind.

FEZILE: Okay then, dear, I'm listening.

NYAMEZO: I think I'm going to quit!

FEZILE: Quit what now!

NYAMEZO: Just this morning I had a terrible experience at the hospital . . .

Transition.

A wordless song while the actors change clothes. A delivery room at the hospital. NYAMEZO *is offstage as a* WHITE SENIOR PAEDIATRICIAN. A WOMAN, *lying on a table, is giving birth.*

NURSE [*to woman*]: C'ammon sisi, push – push – again – push! All right, all right, hold it [*taking scissors to cut umbilical cord.*] Let's see how much it

45

weighs. [*Pause.*] No! 850 grams but it has life – it will live. [*She puts the child in an incubator and goes out shouting.*] Let me rush for the paediatrician. Doctor! Paediatrician! . . .

PAEDIATRICIAN: Yes what is it?

NURSE: We have a premature baby weighing only 850 grams . . . but it's alive!

PAEDIATRICIAN [*peeps out of the half open door*]: Ag, let it die man, it's got no chance anyway! Take that thing to the sluice room.

NURSE: But doctor can't we save it?

The PAEDIATRICIAN *ignores her. A pause.*

NURSE [*to audience*]: One hour later I went to clean the sluice room only to find it gasping for air. [*Speaks to herself*] It's alive! Let me rush for the paediatrician! [*Runs*] Paediatrician! Paediatrician! You've got to resuscitate it please!

PAEDIATRICIAN [*reluctantly*]: Right! I am giving life to this thing and tomorrow it'll be the one that will snatch my bag!

The devastated NURSE *sings.*

Senze ntoni na	What have we done?
Senze ntoni na?	
Senze ntoni na?	
Ho-ho-ho	
Ho-ho-ho	
Senze ntoni na?	
Ho-ho-ho-ho-ho-ho	

Transition.

FEZILE's *home.*

FEZILE: And what happened?

NYAMEZO: The child had already developed hypothermia and it died!

FEZILE [*shattered*]: Hayi man!

NYAMEZO: There were no questions. No investigation and nobody will be taken to task.

FEZILE: What do the nurses say about it?

NYAMEZO: The nurses fear victimisation, all they can do is lament. It is in fact, against the codes of conduct for me to give you this information.

FEZILE [*contemptuously*]: Rubbish! Codes of conduct! The nurses must stand up! The nurses must be organised! All those racists must be pulled out of our hospitals. To hell with racist codes of conduct!

46

NYAMEZO: It's just such a pity . . .

FEZILE: What is a pity?

NYAMEZO: Dr Lumumba has left.

FEZILE: But you are there and every dedicated nurse is there! You should shout in one voice!

NYAMEZO: We cannot, because we do not have a union. The South African Nursing Association would be against it.

FEZILE: That very association consists of racist mentality – how can they take action against their own people? You should form your own union, go for it! Don't be afraid.

NYAMEZO: I won't be. I will go for it!

FEZILE [*encouragingly*]: If you do that, I will be right next to you. And you know what my next step is going to be?

NYAMEZO: Yes, buy another yo-yo!

FEZILE: No ways, my dear . . . I will give up my yo-yo adventures . . . [NYAMEZO *looks surprised*] Can't believe it? It's true. I will give up my yo-yo adventures! [*Grabbing the yo-yo to throw it away, while shouting with* NYAMEZO *close behind him.*]

FEZILE & NYAMEZO: Away with the yo-yo! Away with the yo-yo. Away! *They continue to make a noise back-stage.*

Scene Seven

The hospital. There is a long queue at the Casualty admissions.

QUEUE MARSHALL [*angry at patients*]: Msindo! [*He looks down.*] And now whose card is this! Kha u bheke (Just look!) [*He calls out the name.*] Jonas Magugane! Jonas Magugane c'ammon come for your card. Hurry up! Give him way, let him pass – take! Damn it, you are even in the wrong queue. Don't argue with me ngi zaku phihliza jong (I will clobber you)! [*Threatens to hit him.*] And remember this is not an old age home. Hamba (Go)!

Enter a NURSE *to confront a patient. The patient is imaginary.*

NURSE [*to patient*]: Yes? You come all the way from the gate to ask me questions? Who told you I'm the information officer? You must go back to the enquiries and there you can ask them as many questions as you want. That's what they are there for. [*She turns and freezes with her back towards audience.*]

Enter MAGOGO, *an old woman.*

MAGOGO: We phoyisa (policeman), do you mean I must stand in that long queue?

Q MARSHALL: I can't help it salugazi, you must wake up. Do you think this is the pass office where there is a lot of bribery?

Phone rings. NYAMEZO *still plays nurse.*

SECOND NURSE [*rushing to answer*]: Hallo, hallo! Yes. Can I help you? [*Pause.*] Hi Joey! [*Excitedly*] How are you my lover boy? Oh, I'm fine as usual. What? Pardon, I can't hear you. Just hold on a minute. [*She turns around to scream at a patient.*] You are making noise! I say you are making noise! An old man like you crying from pain? Look at the blood! Are you trying to paint this place red? Rubbish! You must have been drunk when you had that accident! C'ammon move it! [*She turns back to the phone.*] I'm sorry

48

Joey, you know these patients can really drive you up the wall sometimes. Yes. When? Where? Irene's place? Good! We can even to Mosoja's joint. You know I love these two shebeens, they've got a touch of class . . . Yes for people like us. That's why all the visiting superstars are taken there for entertainment . . . the Champion Jack Duprees, the Millie Jacksons and some football team directors enjoy themselves there. Even well known playwrights like Maishe Maponya and Matsemela Manaka also go there for entertainment. Can't we fall under the same class? Good! You are a darling, what do you think I love you for? [*A bit disappointed*] C'ammon Joey you must pick me up. Please Joey fetch me, fetch me Joey? [*Excited again*] I knew you were joking. Now tell me, which car will you be driving? My favourite one? The red Colt Gallant? I love that one . . . Love? I must go now to that boring job you know – come give me a kiss – mba! Mncpwa! [*Dropping the phone and still excited*] Just imagine, Masonja's joint! Lets go dancing oolalaaah!

She dances a bit and freezes with her back to the audience.

MAGOGO: Haaibo! This can't be. Does this suggest that I must queue again just to pay? Why didn't that man take the money at the same time as he gave me the file?

Q MARSHAL: Hey salugazi! You wake up and stop complaining! Uya kompleya, kompleya (You are complaining, complaining)! Ag man!

NYAMEZO *plays another nurse.*

THIRD NURSE [*to another patient*]: Yebo buti can I help you? O you want to go to Ward Fourteen. No problem I can help you. You don't need enquiries. You go straight, turn to your right, you will see red footmarks and they'll lead you to Ward Fourteen . . . Tell me are you sick? I mean with a tie and a suit on, you don't look sick to me. What? This necklace? My grandmother gave it to me [*giggle*] Who me? Thank you, Thank you! [*giggle*] I live in Soweto – Chiawela. I work in this ward. Yes you can visit me at any time . . . Just follow my directions and you won't get lost. Okay, bye-bye. Hope to see you again!

Freezes.

MAGOGO [*to audience*]: After another hour I was told to go to the nurse. I tried to protest. Angizanga kunesi apha, ngifuna udokotela (I've not come to the nurse, I want the doctor).

Q MARSHALL: Salugazi are you still here? Awuguli wena mos! You are not sick! Uzo cheka la! You've come for your boyfriends! Fuck off!

Exit Q MARSHALL

MAGOGO [*to audience*]: I lost the battle and I queued.

NYAMEZO *plays herself and attends to* MAGOGO. A BLACK DOCTOR, *played by* FEZILE, *comes in.*

NYAMEZO [*after looking at* MAGOGO's *file*]: I'm sorry Gogo I can't handle your case. I will refer you to the doctor.

MAGOGO [*exploding*]: I told you I wanted to see a doctor!

NYAMEZO: Gogo this is the procedure here . . .

MAGOGO: Rubbish procedure. It's procedure, procedure everywhere you go. Orderless procedure. [*To audience*] I was now running mad.

B DOCTOR [*to* MAGOGO]: Next please. [*Remembers*] Ah, it's you again Gogo? And what's wrong this time? Pain? Let's see your card. All right, I will prescribe some very good medicine for you. Good. You must go to the chemist and collect your medicine but make sure that you come back here next Monday.

MAGOGO: Doctor you mean I must go and queue again here?

B DOCTOR: No Gogo. This time of day there are not a lot of patients around here. [*She moves out*] No Gogo the chemist is on your right. Next please!

The BLACK DOCTOR *holds the 'Chemist' board and freezes while* MAGOGO *comes to the counter for her medication. A* WHITE PHARMACIST *appears behind the counter.*

PHARMACIST: Come Magogo, let's see. [*He scrutinises the card.*] No, no Magogo go back to your doctor for motivation!

MAGOGO [*confused*]: Usukhuluma ngani manje mntanami (What are you talking about now my child)?

PHARMACIST: I said motivation, motivation Magogo!

She goes to NYAMEZO *for help.*

MAGOGO: Angiyitholanga imithi futhi angiyizwa nale ndoda ekhuluma ngokungishawuda; wozongisiza ntombazana yami (I didn't get the medicine, also I can't understand this man who shouts at me. Come and help me my girl).

NYAMEZO *takes her to the* PHARMACIST.

PHARMACIST: I told her to go for motivation! Motivation Magogo!

NYAMEZO: But Doctor I can't understand this, this is the third patient you have sent back for motivation.

PHARMACIST: And the first two were changed. What's wrong with changing the prescription for this one?

NYAMEZO: Yes, but what I don't understand is that the doctor has actually examined the patient and has prescribed exactly what he knows will cure the patient.

PHARMACIST: I don't dispute that when the patient is young. The old people just waste medicine – they don't take it regularly. Hypertension tablet are very expensive, sister – and you know there is a very low compliance. The follow-up on patients is poor, so why waste expensive medicine? Next please!

Song, led by NYAMEZO

Wozani Manesi	Come nurses
Wezw'e simnyama	Of the black nation
Wozani silweni lomkhuba	Come let's fight these strange goings on
Nxo – Nxo – Nxo	
Kwafa' bantwana	Children die
Imith'ikhona	While medication is there
Wozani silweni lomkhuba	Come let's fight these strange goings on
Nxo – Nxo – Nxo	

NYAMEZO [*to audience*]: A few months later I was called to the local hospital security where I was told . . .

Flashback

LOC SECURITY: Nyamezo, you are organising misconduct amongst the nurses! You are stirring them up! Your behaviour is intolerable and unprofessional. You will be dealt with severely.

End of flashback

NYAMEZO [*to audience*]: And then came the Security Branch to 'take me for a drive'. I was blindfolded and put at the back of the van. And during the 'honeymoon' with the Security Branch I was told in no uncertain terms that . . .

Transition. The two male actors put on white masks and march to confront NYAMEZO. *They stand on either side of her and sing.*

SECURITY BRANCH:

We will panel beat you kaffir
We will panel beat you goed.
Take you to Protea station
Panel beat you
Take you to Modderbee
Leave you naked
Take you to John Vorster Square
Los jou morsdood . . .

We will panel beat you kaffir
We will panel beat you goed.

NYAMEZO: I was told to bring the Health Workers Association constitution which I promised to bring, for I have seen cars being panel beaten. But when I realised I was being turned into an informer, I discussed it with my husband. He was angry with me for offering to assist the police.

CHORUS: In state security!

NYAMEZO: So I never complied. Instead I became brave. We cannot go into battle when we do not expect casualties . . .

A continuation of the song 'Wozani manesi'.

Hey wena vuka	Hey you wake up
Wesaba bani	Who do you fear?
Vukani silweni lomkhuba . . .	Wake up let's fight these strange goings on . . .

Nxo – nxo – nxo

52

Scene Eight

A gathering of the South African Nursing Association (SANA) members. A white official is addressing them. Only the last bits of her speech can be heard. NYAMEZO is present.

OFFICIAL: The South African Nursing Association needs your full support. To bring this body closer to you, we will take another look at the constitution to change it. So far we are very happy with the way things have gone. Our critics have also acknowledged this point . . . And for this reason we must give ourselves a standing ovation! [*Some of the nurses give the speaker a standing ovation.* NYAMEZO *starts ululating and addresses the audience. The other members sit down.*]

NYAMEZO: Liiiiiiwu! liiiiwu! Ngcanda Kwedini agcwal'amancgwaba Umongikazi ebhekile! Ngcanda kwedini agcwal'amancgwaba. Umongikazi ebhekile! Mongikazi wase Afrika! Have you forgotten the day you took your vow? Did you vow to let your people die in front of you? Or are you scared to follow your convictions?

Two patients in a bed for one. Overcrowding! And where do our children get malnutrition in a rich country like ours? No! no! That's nonsense! That's nonsense! We must form our own union. Nurses of Afrika, you are the light you are the life, you are the light you are the life, you are the light you are the life!

Mongikazi omnyama ongubozimhlophe! Floors, floors are beds for dying millions of your people!

Au wena Owavela nokukhanya Kwelanga! There is life in your hands. Resuscitate them to life because you can! It is inevitable that we must now form our own union! The situation here is being reinforced and aggravated by the poorly-qualified so-called doctors – the Taiwanese, the Polish, the Israelis, the Germans and all those chance-takers who could not make it

53

in their countries. This is their Canaan. There is manna here for them. Yes, the authoritarian type of institution is showing its true colours . . .

A MALE NURSE *raises his hand. He gets the approval of the meeting to speak.*

FIRST MALE NURSE: To add to that . . . recently a great number of qualified nurses have been refused permission to practise in the cities. The reason is that it is alleged that they come from the homelands. Ridiculous that this is done at a hospital level!

SECOND MALE NURSE [*interrupting*]: Who cares where a nurse comes from?

MALE NURSE: Now, what I fail to understand is that the hospital also practises influx control! I agree to the formation of a union of the nurses, the doctors, the porters, and all other people who are employed in the hospitals. We are a trade! The hospital is a factory where broken bodies are being mended, you know! Yes, I support the formation of a union!

Applause. SECOND MALE NURSE *stands up.*

SECOND MALE NURSE: Sister Nyamezo, since we are all off duty, I move that we take off these hospital uniforms so that we are not caught off-guard by the 'codes of conduct'.

All-out excitement as everybody starts to undress. They create an image of nurses being trampled upon but rising up. They sing.

Ndithi nyuka nxai ndini   I say rise up you lazy ones
Ndithi nyuka nxai ndini
Ndithi nyuka nxai ndini!

Maishe Maponya

Mark Newman

DIRTY WORK

Dirty Work premiered at The Market Theatre in 1984 in a double bill with *Gangsters*. Jon Maytham played the role of Pieter Hannekom.

The action takes place in a conference room in which Pieter Hannekom is giving a lecture.

TIME: The present

PROPS: Blackboard, duster, table or desk, picture on the wall (preferably of Hendrik Verwoerd), mirror, tape recorder, food and drink containers, briefcase, suit and tie, two army jackets, lappie (or gas mask), army beret.

LIGHTS: General cover with flicker effect for explosions and alternate state (for mimes).

SOUND: Music, explosion, machine-gun fire, street battle noises, laughter, offstage noises of interruption, radio news broadcast.

Enter Piet Hannekom from the auditorium entrance. He is the last person to enter the room. Any late-comer will be subjected to a search by Hannekom who will improvise lines related to security. He wears a gentle smile as he walks to the stage, acknowledging the presence of all delegates to the conference. He places the briefcase on the table, opens it, takes out a file and closes it. Once more he gives the house a gentle smile.

HANNEKOM: Good morning ladies and gentlemen, welcome, dames en here (ladies and gentlemen), welkom. Oh, I see that we have some black delegates from our neighbouring states, Ciskei, Venda, Bophuthatswana, KwaZulu – so manene na manenekazi siyanibulisa. I hope I got that right, I've been practising for weeks. My first and very pleasant duty is to welcome you all here on behalf of our first citizen, the Honourable Prime Minister and his Number One assistant, the Honourable Minister of Defence, to what we hope will be a very exciting, very advanced, very informative and most historic session.

You know, ladies and gentlemen, I am sure that when historians come to write about this time, they will regard this conference as a watershed in the Post-Carlton Centre era maar ons sal die geskiedenis laat besluit nê (but we will let history decide, not so)? Both our honoured patrons send their greetings and their apologies. They had hoped to be here but they are in Switzerland on private financial business and also the British government has given them permission to visit the Falkland Islands in order to lay wreaths in memory of the Boer women and children who died there in concentration camps.

While we are on the subject of our leaders, ladies and gentlemen, I would like us to think about all the unsung heroes of our beloved land, Dr Verwoerd, Dr Malan, Mr Vorster, who we miss in these times of troubles and unrest in the country. I would like to ask you all please to remain silent for fifteen seconds in their memory. [*He bows his head.*]

Thank you. Well, ladies and gentlemen, the newsapers have been speculating for weeks as to who will head the newly-formed Department of

Security. It gives me great pleasure to lay that speculation to rest. I am that man. My name is Pieter Hannekom [*he writes the name on the board*] and I was appointed director of security with specific instructions to reorganise the department along modern technical lines. I was also instructed to restructure the department so as to ensure that all the citizens of this wonderful country can live in peace and security and prosperity and in stability and of course in their own group areas. [*Laughs.*] I was also instructed to establish a functional relationship between the departments of security and defence and the business sector, hence this conference – the first concrete achievement of my department but, I assure you, not the last.

Now, you are probably all sitting there wondering, and quite correctly too, who is this man and what gives him the right to stand up there and lecture us about security? Well my name, as I said before, is Pieter Hannekom and I have a long history of interest in security affairs, which dates back, if I may be forgiven a personal reminiscence, to the age of five. You know ladies and gentlemen, I was in my little kamer en ek het met my . . . well, how shall I put this . . .? I was examining my anatomy in the way that little children do when my mother came in, caught me, and most definitely did not approve en ek het 'n vreeslike pakslae gekry (I got a terrible hiding). I can still feel it. [*Laughs.*] But the point of that little anecdote is that my little mind realised there and then that if one wished to live a peaceful and prosperous life, one had to have controlled access to premises – in other words, one had to have SECURITY [*He writes the word on the board*].

This interest in security continued during my school years. My favourite subjects were science and metalwork and in my final year, I designed a number of locks, one of which, my own particular favourite, was one which spurted out poison gas if a fail-safe mechanism wasn't activated before the lock was opened. This lock was reported by our local newspaper, the *Senekal Advertiser*, one of the few remaining patriotic newspapers in the land, and it brought me to the attention of a group of men who have asked to remain anonymous and they shall do so, and they sponsored my further career which included training in Rhodesia, Israel, Paraguay and Taiwan and a few other friendly countries, which, for security reasons must remain unnamed, and brought me here eventually to talk to you.

As you can see, these travels have given me a very good English accent. By the way, if any of you are interested in finding out more about my locks, my cousin Sarel runs a very good lock factory – the address is in the conference folders you have all been given. Phone Sarel, mention my name and you're sure of a good price. I have a vast reservoir of knowledge and experience and am almost bursting with enthusiasm to install a tough and effective security department in this, our beloved land. I am sure that at the end of this conference which will, as planned, last for seventy-two hours non-stop, you will share my enthusiasm, some of my knowledge and you will be able to pronounce my name – Hannekom.

The title of our session is 'In-House Training Scheme' [*writes it on the board*] which we felt was innocuous enough to deceive even the most suspicious-minded of the liberal newspapers. The object of the session is to transfer ideas and knowledge from me to you. I am sure that you all agree that the encouragement and co-operation between industry members and security agencies will result in a better future for us all.

You know, ladies and gentlemen, if you go into the offices and workplaces today, you will find that when the people are not working, they are not talking about how Zola will do at the next Olympic Games, or whether Ian Botham will agree to play cricket in South Africa, what they are talking about is strikes and boycotts. Strikes and boycotts! [*He writes the words on the board.*]

My cousin Koos, who runs a very good market research agency which you might like to make use of – the address is in your folders – well, Koos has just completed a survey which shows that 86.4 per cent of average white South Africans talk about strikes and boycotts for an average 17.6 minutes on an average day. Now that means that, quite apart from the money lost from the strikes and boycotts themselves, this country loses 300 million rand every year in wasted man hours. The economic prospects of the business are of course well known to you. Now, with the exchange rate of the rand and the price of gold being what they are today, that is a lot of money! And let us not forget the threat of sanctions propounded by our commie-loving friends in the West. Perhaps what you are less aware of is the link between industrial action on the one hand and terrorist action on the other. You know when Mr Slogun and his comrades sit there in their London offices planning their strategies, they don't only plan where to plant a bomb, they also plan where to plant a subversive thought. And this conference will give us ways and means of combating these terror tactics – to allow us all to fulfil the motto of the security department which is

cause bella hic haec hoc Russki excreta
Terra firma propatria bellis securita!

Which, for those of you who are not versed in the classical languages roughly translates as:

Let us resist the community through manure
Let us fight for our land and be secure!

And that brings me to a very very important point; you know it is my contention and the contention of my colleagues that in recent years the image of the security agencies has not been what it should have been, but we plan to change all that. What we have done is we have identified key security concerns and we have had songs written about those concerns by some of South Africa's foremost recording artists. Luckily a relative of mine is head of a well-known stereo radio service so we are assured that our records will go to the top of the hit parade and thus have enormous impact. For example, the very important link between industrial action and terrorist action which I spoke about earlier has been put into a song which goes, and I beg forgiveness in advance if I make Boy George sound like Champion Jack Dupree but here goes [*puts his hands together and stands in an upright position*]

Boycott sabotage
Boycott sabotage
Go together like strikes and hand grenades . . .

[*He stops in the middle of the song, embarrassed at his own discord.*]

Well, if it's done properly it sounds very good and we are sure that the strategy will be effective and will have just the impact we want. Now, you have all been notified to bring food parcels and flasks of non-intoxicating liquors. For security reasons you will not be permitted to leave these premises until the conference ends in [*looks at his watch*] 71 hours and 51 minutes time and I hope for your peace of mind and the comfort of your stomachs that you have in fact done so – and I am sure that I don't have to explain the function of the glass bottles you have all been issued with. As you can see I am very well prepared. I am lucky that my wife's cousin's brother-in-law's father has a very nice fast food delicatessen. It's open 24 hours a day – the address is in your folders. And perhaps as a final remark in this introductory section I might just mention that in case of fire, do not panic. There is a water tower on the top of this building which circulates four thousand four hundred gallons of water a minute, and I'm sure that you have all mastered the simple sport of swimming. [*Surveys the audience.*] Oh dear, I can see from your reaction that this is in fact not so. Well never mind, I have some lifesavers here! [*Big laugh*] No, it's only a joke. I was just trying to lighten the atmosphere a little. Ha-ha-ha! Seriously though ladies and gentlemen, in case of fire I am sure that you all agree that a properly-designed fire detection system coupled with a properly-working fire extinguishing system will ensure that this conference proceeds entirely without hitches . . .

Lights flicker and go out.

O Here, ons is in die donker (Oh Lord, we are in the dark). Ligte man! Ladies and gentlemen, there seems to be some small electrical problem. This is the first occurance of its kind in any conference I've had. I'm sorry I'll have to go and see what the problem is. Why not have a Coke and a smile and I shall soon have the current working again. You just listen to the music. [*Switches on the tape on his table . . . music, for example 'Noddy goes to space'.*] I'll be back with you in a moment.

Exits. Enters again after a short while. He's got a beret on his head and is carrying a handgun.

Well here I am again. You know ladies and gentlemen the black youths of today don't have quite the same respect for education that we used to have. The little buggers have set fire to the distribution board at their school, hence the electricity problem. But they've learned a different kind of lesson today and even if they won't be able to sit down for a while, they are back at school. [*There is distant verbal abuse off-stage. He shudders and quickly collects himself.*] There's nothing to worry about ladies and gentlemen it's a cultural problem, the blacks don't know how to talk in a whisper. Well let us continue with the conference. You know ladies and gentlemen, most of you, excuse me a moment . . . [*He takes the gun and goes to the door, looks out, comes back.*] As I was saying, most of you have been relying up until now on the Human Access Control System – HACS. [*Writes it on the board.*] We in the department of security feel that this system has become unsatisfactory for a number of reasons.

Firstly, their union, the Union of Guards Human UGH [*writes the abbreviation on the board*] has become very unreasonable in their demands, they're pricing themselves quite out of the market. And some of their demands for improved working conditions are ridiculous. What do they want to do with twelve days a year holiday. The whole bloody job is a holiday! And this other demand of theirs that they be allowed to patrol and work in pairs – it's ridiculous for many reasons besides the extra expense, they probably just want to chatter on about soccer and horse racing and the strange things that take place in their shebeens.

64

Another cause for our dissatisfaction is that they become less efficient as the evening wears on. Their alertness deteriorates in proportion to the number of cartons of home made brew they drink. Also, let us face facts ladies and gentlemen, one of these guards would at best be a minor hindrance to anyone bent on serious mayhem. After all, the struggle of the knobkierie versus the machinegun is about as unequal as a carton of 'shake-shake' (sorghum beer) and a bottle of gin – maar ons sal nie daaroor praat nie (but we won't talk about that). The only way out of this impasse would be to arm these security guards but that would mean that an unsophisticated sector of the population would have access to sophisticated weaponry which they are not trained to use – a dangerous prospect.

Another problem which you might not have thought of – you know in large industrial businesses a large segment of the labour force chooses not to eat in the canteens which have been provided for them, but choose instead to take their own meat stews and putu porridge or mphokoqo or whatever you call it. It then becomes quite possible for a saboteur to smuggle hand grenades and plastic explosives inside these food parcels and for a guard to search through all this would be very time consuming not to mention messy. My cousin Transvaal, who is a senior official at the Rand Water board, calculated that even if a guard were only to wash his hands after every fourth search, a force of five men at a plant like SASOL VI would consume 119 000 gallons of water daily and in these dry times that is a lot of water! Here hey, die droog is daarm erg (Lord, the drought is really bad). I couldn't get a decent swim the whole summer with all these restrictions on filling my pool, can you believe me?

There is a sudden bang offstage. HANNEKOM *reacts. He is slightly embarrassed by his reaction and tries to keep calm.*

Well, ladies and gentlemen, despite these drawbacks there is still one situation in which the human guard is of great use. I refer of course to the roadblock situation. You know with these townships being such a hotbed of intrigue and terror it often becomes necessary to monitor and search people coming in and going out along with all the improved emergency traffic. I'll give you a little demonstration.

[*Sound of car hooters. Lights change,* HANNEKOM *mimes a search.*]

Right! All the cars drop the people – we'll search the people and search the cars and the people get back to your cars and drive off! [*Hooters.*] And shut up! There's no need to make such a bloody noise! We'll get to you in a moment! Right, everybody out of the cars!

[*More hooters.*]

Hey toela man, shut up, julle kaffirs het nie maniere nie (you kaffirs have no manners)! Why are you making such a noise? You are going to a wedding? I didn't know you people got married. All right out of the car. Whew! What a wedding dress. I'm not going to search through all those layers. Geoff, give me the metal detector [*He walks around the woman. There's a pip-pip sound.*] It's all right Geoff that's only her metal coil. Well, it doesn't look like you're concealing anything except the fact that you're no longer a virgin bride. Right, the men up against the car. [*He searches a man, and finds a cake*] You're supposed to eat the wedding cake afterward not before . . . [*He looks at the cake and decides to eat it.*] Right, back in the car and drive on! Next! Come out of the car! [*Searches another man.*] Hey Geoff, Jim was right about what *Scope* Magazine said about black men. Okay Errol Flynn, back in the car. Ag man this is getting boring. I'm going to have a little fun. [*He stops the next car and walks around it.*] Nee jong this looks a suspicious car. [*Fast and impatient*] Drive it over there! Jack it up, take off all the wheels, take out all the seats, remove the engine, open the boot, we're going to have a proper search. Hey kaffir what do you mean I don't have the right to do that, dit en dit gee my die reg. Nou trek die kar soontoe (this and this give me the right. Now pull the car over there)! Geoff look after this bloke. [*Turns around and sees another car*] Whew! Dis nou 'n motor kar. BMW 635 CSI – mag wheels, spoiler, kiwi fruit on the aerial [*looks inside*] hey manne – die kaffir het 'n telefoon en 'n TV in sy kar (the kaffir has a telephone and a TV in his car). Wragtig (truly)! You must own a shebeen to have a car like this hey? Ag no, I don't need to search you. Just drive on. [*He looks at his watch.*] Hey Paul, I must fetch my wife from the Greek dance lessons. Sien jou more oggend by Atteridgeville. Julle bring die brandewyn die keer julle suinige moers (See you tomorrow morning in Atteridgeville. This time you bring the brandy you stingy bastards)! [*Laughs.*]

Lights change to general.

So that ladies and gentlemen, deals with the human guard access control system. What we at the Department of Security would rather suggest is that you investigate, [*writes on board*] remove the gate and invest in electronic security systems. Now, as you'll see from your conference folders, this subject will be covered later on by an AV, which, for those of you who are feeling concerned and confused does refer to an audio visual and not the Afrikaner Volkswag. [*Laughs like a drain.*] But seriously, ladies and gentlemen, I would like to make a few remarks now. You know there is a wide range of equipment available on the market, but I would like to refer you to two systems that were developed here in South Africa in the Department of Industrial Machinery at the University of Machadodorp by a research team led by my uncle Professor Gerd Hannekom. Now the first has the technical name [*writes on board*] TVS MARK IV, but is more affectionately known as 'search but not destroy'. It works on the same principle as those machines that you put your bags through at airports and at the SABC and such places except that this one has been programmed to respond vocally. So, for example, you have a terrorist who's just dismantled an AK47 and he has hidden all the parts inside loaves of bread. 'n Kaffir maak altyd 'n plan (a kaffir always makes a plan). He's now got all those loaves of bread in one of those baker's trays. He's coming into your building to shoot you all to pieces. He looks very casual. [*Whistles as he mimes the action. The warning sound on the machine goes off. He freezes in frustration.*]

Taped sound: This nasty man is carrying the components of an AK47. Remove him.

At that moment the floor opens and he falls into the cell below. Smart hey? The other progress that has been made is in the field of Hominoid Unique Featurisation – HUF. [*Writes the abbreviation on the board.*] I am sure that you all know dames en here, that people's fingerprints are unique, and some of you might know that the pupils of people's eyes react differently to light. What Professor Gert and his team have discovered is the fascinating information that the back of everybody's knee is different. No two people have the same back of knee. No ladies and gentlemen, this is not the time to start looking at your knees – time has been set aside for that later on. So if you want to control access to your premises, all you have to do is require everybody who might have legitimate access to undergo a kneeprint anglogram and then the machine can recognise him or not.

Of course there is one small problem, though, you know gentlemen these days wear tight trousers, so it becomes a hassle for them to lift up their trousers to find the knee . . . and women who are hiding their varicose veins and those who cut their legs while shaving would be very embarrassed if they were made to reveal those ugly sights to the world. But once again the Hannekom family has a solution! My cousin Louis, on my mother's side that is – Louis on my father's side is the bloody sucker of the family. He's just opened up another fatcake and biltong joint in Dallas. But Louis on my mother's side has designed a range of very exciting fashionable clothes which all have a transparent flap patched at the back of the knee. So all you do is walk up to the machine [*he demonstrates*], present the knee and if the machine recognises you, then in you go, but if it doesn't, down you go into the pit below!

Laughter offstage. There is a panicky reaction from HANNEKOM, *then he, too, laughs, weakly.*

I wonder what's amusing old Johannes now? That's the tea boy. A remarkable sense of humour for someone who is over 60.

Anyway, another very useful piece of electronics system is electronic surveillance, both overt and covert. Now most of you will probably think that video surveillance is only used for crime prevention and detection, but it can also be very useful in morality surveillance and industrial control. All you have to do is put concealed microphones and cameras in the places where workers gather in their off-duty times and you will soon find out who the trouble makers are and you can deal with them accordingly. We were also doing very nicely with video cameras in detainees' cells, done entirely for their protection, until the liberal press got hold of it and made a mountain out of a molehill. Some people will do anything to make a fuss!

On morality ladies and gentlemen we are quite conscious of how many of you go to those X-rated films at Sun City. A very useful side effect of having an extensive video surveillance system is assisted by the statistically proven rate of sexual encounter between workers. For those of you who are interested, the well-known TV producer Eric Hannekom, no relation, has compiled a selection of scenarios which are available on VHS, Beta and Philips. I mean, if you put cameras in enough broomcupboards and boardrooms, you will see some very interesting sights, there are black men with black women, white men with white women, a black man with a white woman, a white man and a black woman, a black poof and a white poof – various combinations of the above and in one particularly memorable instance – a managing director with a Doberman Pinscher; imagine the AIDS!

[*Sounds of explosions and related noise offstage. Lights flicker.*]

Excuse me please, I will just go and see what the noise is about.

[*He exits, turning on the music tape as he goes. Returns a minute later.*]

A few isolated trouble-makers but they have been dealt with.

[*Drinks water. Looks at notes.*]

Well I see from our schedule that I have planned some relaxation time. So I suggest that we put it to use by playing a game; not just any game but one that will have direct relevance to this conference.

[*Cleans the board.*]

Let's take our title 'In-house training scheme' and I will select a word at random. 'House' Okay? Who can give me a word associated with 'House'? Yes? Key! Very good. Now what do we use a key for – unlocking the door and getting in. Well done. In-house – we have a link. Now 'in' is a very important word. Can anybody give me examples of words beginning with in: [*Takes words from audience, writing them on the blackboard as he goes.*]

'Independence' – everyone who co-operates with us will be given their independence. 'Incendiary' – as in incendiary tactics, as practised by the ANC, PAC and SWAPO. 'Internal' – excellent! Internal security is vital to our co-existence. 'Intercourse' – no really madam at your age. 'Intimidate' – that's what I call a good word – as in intimidating the workers of Soweto. 'Invade' – [*he seems to have difficulty writing it*] no, I don't like that word. Let's ignore it and move on to the next word in our title. Training – now what can we link training with – 'uniform' – well done – we are moving fast. Training can be linked to uniform. If you are a Karateka and you want to go training, you put on a uniform and then people know who you are and respect you. In fact, to expand on this slightly, the law making committee of the Security Council are at present favourably considering a proposal of mine. I suggested that everybody in the country be divided into one of 134 categories and that a uniform be designed for each of those categories which the members (of those categories) will be required by law to wear. It is my feeling that somebody who is unemployed because he is lazy will be ashamed of wearing the unemployed uniform and he will go out and find work. So I feel the uniform bill will increase economic productivity.

[*Pause. Looks at the board.*]

Well we have a fine collection of words here. Independence, incendiary, inter-of-course intimidate, invade

[*Stops.*] Excuse me ladies and gentlemen. [*Goes to a corner. Screams.*] Invade! Invade, that's better. Doctor's orders I'm sorry. I suffer from a condition that doctors call psychosomatic. Whenever I say certain words my stomach tightens and I can only loosen it by screaming the word out of my system. Invade. Nothing to be worried about, nobody is going to invade us.

[*Lights flicker. Sound of machine-gun fire. He rushes for his gun.*]

Just listen to the music.

[*He switches on the tape. Exits. Returns after a while wearing a lappie or gas-mask. He is exhausted and has a bleeding gash on his forehead. The sleeve and part of the jacket are torn and bloodstained. He has difficulty in breathing normally. He explains.*]

A few isolated trouble makers but they've been dealt with.

[*Pause.*]

Oh, perhaps I should tell you about this. It's a very useful security accessory. The lappie is just an ordinary one that you can buy at the OK or Pick 'n Pay and there are moves afoot to have them tax-exempted. And it comes in a range of twelve very fashionable colours. What makes it special is this fluid which was invented by Professor Gert and his team called tri-chloro-polymethutoluene-baking-bean or some such thing. If there is industrial unrest at your plant, then you put it on and it stops the tear gas from getting at you. So what you do is, you put the fluid over the lappie and put the lappie over your nose and put your nose over the steering wheel of an RP and you're all fine. Of course you don't know what an RP is? I'm sorry I should have told you. An RP is a vehicle. It stands for Riot-Pacifier and it is very useful in controlling political and related labour riots . . . And we get it from the United States. Why the United States? Well, because they are our friends, like us, they have Russia as their number one enemy. The Americans want to help us stop the Russians from transforming this land into chaos! Anyway these machines have a kind of PA system on top with which you can tell the rioters to shut up. And if this doesn't work they've got machines that fire rubber bullets and a sort of pod which farts out – I beg your pardon, it poeps, oh I'm sorry which emits a very powerful tear gas and then all the rioters run around like headless chickens [*Laughter*]. Seriously though, if you have any unrest in your factories or whatever, these machines will sort them out quickly enough. Of course they can only be bought with a permit but I have a cousin in the permit department and there should be no problem. You might well need these machines, ladies and gentlemen, because rest assured, you have communists in your businesses. But you mustn't worry because they are easy to identify. If a communist has a headache and wants an aspirin, he will come to you and talk of aspirations so that you can have the headache. [*Roars of laughter.*] Seriously ladies and gentlemen, a terrorist is easy to identify!

If he scratches slogans on his coffee mugs – beware!

If he reads the liberal press – take care!
If he listens to that long hair rasta music
Linton Kwesi Johnson, Bob Tosh, Peter Marley
watch out for him
And if he belongs to a union
Take double care!

Because we have incontrovertible proof that unions are nothing other than fronts for banned organisations ... And I tell you ladies and gentlemen, we are not far from declaring a State of Emergency in all trade unions.

If any of you think that the enemy is still in Russia you are walking in your sleep – I repeat you are walking in your sleep. The enemy is all around! The enemy is all around. He could be sitting right next to you.

[*Sound of machine-gun.* HANNEKOM *jumps up in a panic. He explains his reaction.*]

Just a demonstration of how highly trained we are in security. If there is a stimulus we give a response.

Well I've been telling you what to do about security and you're probably wondering what the government is doing for your security.

[*Shouting from offstage*: VIVA AZANIA! *He looks about in panic and, collecting sandbags, he starts to build a sandbag fortress.*]

I had planned to do a sandbag fortress demonstration later on but with the forces of darkness drawing nearer I might as well do it now.

In the highly unlikely, I say unlikely because we have everything under control, in the unlikely event of your home coming under attack, then you can do what I am doing. I'm doing this for the sole purpose of demonstration.

What the government is doing for your security is passing lots and lots and lots of laws. In 1965, the beloved Honourable Very Right Mr Hendrik Verwoerd, may peace be upon him, established a committee to identify all industrial installations which were thought to have strategic value. But a year later he died an untimely and undignified death before he could complete his great work, he died an undignified death by a knife right in the middle of parliament and the effort was continued under the chairmanship of the honourable B J Vorster, of beloved memory, who handled the upsurge of riots with care, may peace be upon him too, but he too had his career interrupted by the forces of darkness in the form of Muldergate, termed by the liberal press the Information Scandal and the work was completed by the brilliant triumvirate of Bothas. The key achievement of their work, if you will excuse the pun, was the passing of the National Key Points Act, by which they identified more than one thousand key points in this country which have to be protected. All of you present here today have a business in one of these areas and it is obvious that you need security despite my best efforts. I am taking no chances. I am taking security measures, security because you are vulnerable to sabotage and attack.

[*Short machine-gun fire. Lights flicker.* HANNEKOM *dives behind the sandbags. Pause. He peeps out. Pause.*]

I'm sorry ladies and gentlemen I had forgotten that the local Skiet Kommando has their shooting practice every evening just around the corner. Ladies and gentlemen, in the highly unlikely event – contrary to the communist propaganda we are still in charge – in the unlikely event of direct armed confrontation, we have things we can do. So as an example, you could disperse the army and police into all townships and get reinforcement from the homelands. They will always be at the ready to help us deal with those who want to overthrow our state by violent means. And as you do these things you must declare a state of emergency and disperse the 32 Battalion around the townships; remember we have not yet tested their might. [*Pause.*] I declare this place an Operational Area [*Writes the words on the blackboard.*] These are times of crisis ladies and gentlemen. In times of crisis censorship must be applied. Another example, I place a banning order on the use of the blackboard. [*Writes 'banned' across the board. Looks around suspiciously and turns the blackboard back to front.*] The blackboard is banned! I am taking no chances. I am taking security measures. [*Sits on sandbags and aims the gun at the audience.*] Well let us continue with the conference.[*The lights flicker and remain at 50 percent. There is the noise of a pitched street battle. He jumps behind the sandbags and continues his address at the top of his voice as fast as he can.*]

Military and paramilitary forces are becoming increasingly important in State Security. Commandos have been formed comprising conscripts who have finished their twenty-four month national service, soon to be increased to thirty-six. They are highly trained and lightly equipped like an infantry parabat troop. They have both black and white soldiers, but you mustn't worry because the blacks come from the homelands and we have signed agreements with their leaders saying that we can use them in the front lines. So that if anybody tries to invade us . . .

[*The word 'invade' seems to choke him. He has a heart attack. As he falls dying on top of the sandbags a news programme is heard*]

72

NEWSREADER: Good evening. The time is six o'clock and the news is read
by Victor Frederickse:

Zola Budd has returned to South Africa for a two week holiday after her
recent double gold victory at the Olympic Games.

The office of the Prime Minister has announced that the newly created
Department of Security has just held a conference which was designed to
inform businessmen from South Africa and neighbouring independent states
about matters affecting their well-being and security. The conference was
conducted by department head Piet Hannekom. The conference was, ac-
cording to Mr Hannekom's secretary, a great success. It ran smoothly and
there was a frank and fruitful exchange of views. Mr Hannekom was not
available for comment.

The Prime Minister arrived back from his overseas holiday today, where
he had lunch with the Honourable Prime Minister of Great Britain, Mrs
Margaret Thatcher, and was welcomed by a five hundred and forty-two
gun salute at DF Malan Airport . . .

Blackout

Maishe Maponya in the original production of *Gangsters*

GANGSTERS

The original production of *Gangsters* premiered at the Market Theatre, Johannesburg in 1984 as part of a double bill with *Dirty Work*. WHITEBEARD was played by Jon Maytham, JONATHAN by Sol Rachilo and RASECHABA (in that production a male poet) by Maishe Maponya.

The play was restricted by the Director of Publications under the Publications Act of 1974: Public Entertainment and could not be performed in South Africa without the approval of the Publications Control Board.

This version premiered at the Lincoln Centre, New York in 1986 with WHITEBEARD played by Anthony 'Speedo' Wilson, JONATHAN by George Lamola and MASECHABA by Nomathemba Mdini.

GANGSTERS was originally published in the United States in a collection of South African plays entitled *Woza Afrika* (Brazillier Publications). It has been performed in South Africa, the United Kingdom and the United States. There is however a vast difference in performance style between the original text and this one.

The poem 'Ridovhakunda Ridovhavulaya' by Dumakude ka-Ndlovu in the original text has been replaced by 'Hoyini!' written by the author.

Cast

MAJOR WHITEBEARD a white Security Police Officer

JONATHAN a black Security Policeman

MASECHABA a poet

SETTING: The stage is divided into two acting areas, stage left and stage right, by lighting or other means. Stage right is a security cell. Stage left represents Major Whitebeard's office and various settings. Additional lighting needed is a blue cover (for the recitation of poems) and a special, used twice only. The transitions between these states are marked in the text.

PROPS: Slab or stretcher, table, two chairs, cell window bars, blanket (black), rope (two metres), two tape recorders (one small, one large), note pad and pen, one Bible, a briefcase, books, papers, two photographs, a gun and holster, handcuffs. Unforms for JONATHAN and WHITEBEARD, veil for MASECHABA, clothes and gown (mourning) for MASECHABA.

SOUND: A taped hymn.

Prologue

House lights off. Stage lights off. House lights slowly come up to 50 per cent as MASECHABA *enters the auditorium.*

The recitation of the first three poems should take place in the auditorium suggesting a public performance by the poet. The reading must not be in a rigid stationary position, the poet must move in any direction she wishes, through the seats of the auditorium, walking and sometimes running, depending on the mood in each poem. It is also important to note that the tempo varies from one poem to the other and therefore requires the poet to be flexible.

MASECHABA:

Kutheni na mawethu
that you leave the evil fires
from Europe to spread through Afrika!

Sisi Phithiphithi!
Our children lie dead in the streets
whilst their fathers die
digging the gold
they will never smell.

Sisi Wiliwili!
Gugulethu is no longer ours
Sophiatown is no more
e-Mgababa ziya phel'izindlu ngo mlilo

There are no roads e-Crossroads
And our heroes
Are buried in Sharpeville.

Izwe liya nyikima!
Zi ya phel'ingane nga-mabhunu

They still refuse to swallow Bantu Education
Ncedani Mawethu
They are your children.

Izwe liya shukuma!
Nobody can buy apartheid
Rent is going up!
Food is also expensive
Asinamali we cannot afford it.

[*Lights come up to 30 per cent on Major Whitebeard's office revealing* WHITEBEARD *on a chair at a table and* JONATHAN *adjacent to* WHITE-BEARD. *They are both reading newspapers.*

Kutheni na mawethu
That you leave the stranger
To beat the drums of war
In your own backyards!
Hlanganani mawethu!
Lelethu!

[*She pauses as she contemplates the audience and then continues with another poem.*]

Ugly brown canvas uniform
Have you had lunch today?
I have seen
Your contorted face
Behind an ugly brown truck
In Sharpeville again

Ugly brown canvas uniform
I thought I saw your cousin
Behind an ugly brown truck
That roams the streets
By day in Mamelodi

My brother wrote me a letter
And told me about a mean looking face
In Nyanga
Behind an ugly brown truck

And I bet you
It sounds like your brother

Other people too
In Katlehong
In Huhudi
In Leandra
Say they live in fear of
Ugly brown canvas uniforms
Behind ugly brown trucks

And when at night
I smell cyanide in the air
I twitch my nose
Helplessly acknowledging
·The announcement of the air
'Life must be short for others'

And in the morning
When I walk the same streets
In Sharpeville again
I see mothers kneeling beside bodies
Riddled with bullets
And I mutter to myself
The ugly brown truck
Drives a maneater
Dressed in ugly brown canvas uniform

[*She pauses, then continues with a third poem.*]

You puzzle me Mister Gunslinger
To think you will be strong enough
To rid your conscience
Of the days you made our lives ugly

With torture
With blood
With massacre

Mister Gunslinger
Are you really sure
You understand why you suppress
Our aspirations

And our dreams
Into nightmares

Mister Gunslinger
Are you aware of the deeds
Of your settler-forebears
With their wagon-wheels
Running
And crushing
The blooming lives
Cuddled with hope

You with your brown bombers
Ugly as ever
Parading the streets
Like it is the bush
Instilling fears into old folks
Cannot do the same
To the young determined
Azanians

Grandmothers!
Daughters of the living cradle
Summon your gods
In all Afrika
And let it be known
The realities of history are today

Settler child
You defended your
Vile interests
With the blood of my brother
You broom-flying witch
Afrika knows your kind

All ye black shadows
Very darkness of
The gunslingers' high noon
Awake and break open
The gates of the Azanian morning

Grope dear children
Waggle your fingers

Grab the pole
And raise the flag
Drenched in blood
And give us a song
For this victory!

[*With her hands raised and fists clenched in a black power salute she shouts her last lines as she walks backwards out of the auditorium*]

Amandla to the people!
Amandla to the people!

First Encounter

Lights at full on Whitebeard's office. WHITEBEARD *and* JONATHAN *are still seated in the same positions.*

WHITEBEARD: Jonathan!

JONATHAN: Yes sir.

WHITEBEARD: Has someone gone to fetch the poet?

JONATHAN: Yes sir, Sergeant Ngobese has gone to fetch her.

WHITEBEARD: All right. [*Pause. He pages through the newspaper to the end.*]

I see Kaizer Chiefs are playing Orlando Pirates on Saturday – who do you think is going to win?

JONATHAN: Of course it goes without saying, it will be Orlando Pirates all the way – it's like I see it happening again. Exactly what happened in 1973 when they collected all the titles. They are the darlings of our soccer in black and white. [*He throws down the paper, excitedly and mimics.*] Nang'u Rhee! Nang'u Jomo Sono! There's Rhee and Jomo Sono is close behind him . . . Rhee dribbles past two defenders . . . one man lies sprawling on the ground! Rhee passes the ball to Jomo Sono . . . walibamba umfana wa likhahlela! [*Kicks with one leg.*] Laduma! It's a goal!

WHITEBEARD [*interrupting*]: Jonathan!

JONATHAN [*freezes, leg still in the air*]: Yes sir!

WHITEBEARD: Fetch the poet.

JONATHAN: Yes sir! (*Shouts out* MASECHABA's *name.* MASECHABA *walks in slowly. She notes the tape recorder on* WHITEBEARD's *desk. She stops.*]

WHITEBEARD [*folds the newspaper and stands up*]: Miss Masechaba? [*He mispronounces the name.*]

MASECHABA [*correcting him*]: Masechaba is my name.

83

WHITEBEARD: Oh, I'm sorry Miss Masechaba – Major Whitebeard is my name . . . security. [*Produces an identification document.*]

MASECHABA: Yes, what can I do for you?

WHITEBEARD: Miss Masechaba, we in the branch are a little worried about your poetry. We feel it's inflammatory.

MASECHABA: Can you explain yourself? What do you mean?

WHITEBEARD: I don't have to explain myself. All I have to do is to play one of the cassettes that we've got of you reciting those poems – particularly the one called . . . [*recalling*] 'The Spirit of Nation'. All I have to do is play one of the video tapes we've made of you doing your poetry at Regina Mundi commemorative services. That's explanation enough of what I mean. Oh, I'm forgetting my manners, please sit down. [*Offers her a seat.*] Let me get one thing clear for myself. Do you write as well as perform these poems?

MASECHABA: Yes I do.

WHITEBEARD: Don't you feel they are inflammatory?

MASECHABA: They're not.

WHITEBEARD: They're not inflammatory?

MASECHABA: No.

WHITEBEARD: So Miss Masechaba, when you stand in front of a hall full of people, and you've just recited one of your poems and the people start screaming and waving their fists in the air . . . you don't feel it's your poetry that's caused them to react like that?

MASECHABA: No.

WHITEBEARD: That interests me. It interests me . . . [*He looks at* JONA-THAN.] I don't think we need you any longer Jonathan. Why don't you get yourself a cup of coffee. [JONATHAN *leaves.* WHITEBEARD *switches off the tape.*]

MASECHABA: So you have been taping all this?

WHITEBEARD: Regulations, I'm afraid. That's why I got rid of Jonathan. I wanted to have an off-the-record chat with you and I didn't want him to report me upstairs for breaking the rules.

But Miss Masechaba, it really interests me that a woman as obviously intelligent and sensitive as you, can actually believe that your poetry and the reaction it evokes are unrelated? How does the whole thing work?

MASECHABA: You see Major, the manner in which I write my poetry is decided by the situation and inspiration at a given time. Major, when a poet pens anything on paper and the spirit of nature moves within her, she will write about nature. If the spirit of the nation moves within her, she will write about the nation. She will talk about botho, humanness, she'll talk about pain and she'll talk about that which moves the people at a given time. If her people live in happiness, this happiness will be seen in her works; and that will be evidence to the world of how marvellous the lives of her people are. If I don't feel anything, I don't write anything.

WHITEBEARD: Very interesting Miss Masechaba, but that doesn't explain the militant style that you've chosen.

MASECHABA: Major, a poet sees things not in the manner that you and your colleagues see them. You may regard their world as fantasy, but it is in that abstract frame of mind that things start to take a certain shape and form, and that shape is influenced by the material that inspires the poet; hence the manner that I express myself in my poetry.

WHITEBEARD: Very good and very informative. [*Sighs.*] But unfortunately as you yourself put it, my colleagues and I see things differently from you and your people. We live in a different world; far from your abstract frames of mind. So what interests us is not so much the creative process as the effect that your poetry has on ordinary people: people who don't have the insight and understanding that you and I have, and therefore there can be no doubt Miss Masechaba that your poems have made a lot of people feel very angry, even violent and it is my job to put a stop to that sort of thing. So I called you in to have a friendly chat with you and to warn you . . .

MASECHABA: But you talk about violence! I think it's your frame of mind. Maybe it's guilt.

WHITEBEARD: But your poetry is responsible for the creation of a violent frame of mind in the people who hear it . . .

MASECHABA: I am not responsible for the creation of the squatters. I am not responsible for the starvation of millions of children because their parents have been forced into arid homelands. I did not create the humiliating laws, and I never created the racial barriers in this land. Who do you expect me to blame when life becomes unfair to a black soul?

[*No response. Lights fade leaving* MASECHABA *covered by blue light for poem.*]

When life becomes unfair to a black soul
Who is to blame?
When a child leaves home for school never to come back
When a mother hides the cracks on her face created by years of crying.

85

When a brother dashes in fear to seek refuge in the wilderness
We are all taken by surprise!
When life becomes unfair to a black soul
Who is to blame?
When a child throws a stone in anger and dies!
When a family takes a brazier into a shack and dies!
We are all taken by surprise.
But God is not at all taken by surprise!

[*Blue light fades as general lights come up.* MASECHABA *turns challengingly to the Major.*]

Who do you expect me to blame?

WHITEBEARD: Okay, Miss Masechaba, for the purposes of this discussion I will agree that things are not perfect with your people, and this government is doing everything within realistic terms to improve their situation. But you as a poet have a responsibility to your people. I don't know why you choose to depress them by concentrating on the negative aspects of their life. Why don't you cheer them up by talking about the good things that surround them – by telling them of the natural beauty that surrounds them. I'm not an expert of course but I had to learn one poem at school which has stuck in my mind. It goes something like this:

[*He recites any Afrikaans poem about flowers or nature. At the end of his recitation, he goes to lean on the table directly opposite* MASECHABA *and challenges her.*]

Now that sort of poem Miss Masechaba has a beautiful melody to it and it makes me feel good inside not violent and angry.

MASECHABA: Of course I could write about flowers. But where are the flowers in Winterveld for me to write about? What kind of flowers will ever grow in Crossroads? [*Daringly walks to the table, leans on it in the same position as his.*]

If that poet of yours lived in Alexandra he would write about the stagnant pools of water and the smell of shit filtering through the streets at night because there is no drainage system! He would write about the buckets of faeces placed in the streets at night as if families are bragging which family eats more to shit more!

WHITEBEARD: I don't think we need that kind of language Miss Masechaba!

MASECHABA: And my people don't need that kind of life Major Whitebeard.

There is tension as they look each other in the eye.

WHITEBEARD: All right. Let's get back to your poetry. [MASECHABA *goes back to her seat.*]

Can't you see that you are inciting people to violence with your poetry. When you use lines like 'the barbed wire mentality of a good-looking Afrikaner' you are insulting the Afrikaner people. When you write about the 'trigger-happy fingers' it shouldn't surprise you when the people respond by raising their fists in the air and shouting 'Amandla Ngawethu!'

MASECHABA [*standing to make her point*]: But you have just directed your . . .

WHITEBEARD: Yes Miss Masechaba! [*Points to the chair. Then softer.*] It's been a very interesting discussion. But the fact remains that I have a job to do and that job is to warn you. [*Goes to stand behind the chair on which* MASECHABA *is seated.*]

You are playing with fire. And remember my friend that people who play with fire must expect to get burned. If you want to continue playing with fire, don't blame anyone when you get those poetry-writing fingers of yours burned. Well, thank you very much for coming to this chat with me. You may go.

There is tension as MASECHABA *stands to leave the room.*

WHITEBEARD [*calls out*]: Jonathan!

JONATHAN [*comes in*]: Yes sir!

WHITEBEARD: Give me the tape. [JONATHAN *goes to some corner in the office and produces a small tape recorder which he passes to him.* WHITEBEARD *makes a mark on the tape and puts it away.*]

I want you to keep an eye on Masechaba. This means, Jonathan, that you do not go to Ellis Park to watch the soccer match on Saturday. I want you to do a good job. Do you hear me Jonathan?

JONATHAN [*disappointed*]: Yes sir.

The church. A hymn. Suggest that Bach or Mozart should be played softly during this scene. Suggest the acting area should be downstage centre. MASECHABA *enters dressed for church. She crosses herself, finds a place and goes to kneel down. Hymn continues.* JONATHAN *enters, Bible in hand. Finds a place and kneels. Crosses himself and looks about. He sees her and shuffles about to get closer to her. She sees him. He kneels immediately behind her. A little later she challenges him. They talk in whispers.*

MASECHABA: Jonathan, is there anywhere one can go without you following one?

JONATHAN [*sarcastically*]: Yes. The toilet.

87

MASECHABA: No Jonathan, this is serious. I am getting irritated at the manner in which you keep following me. What is it you want from me?

JONATHAN [*amused*]: You must be exaggerating. What makes you such an expert on the Special Branch? Anyway, what would I find to do here besides attending the church service?

MASECHABA: You should be ashamed of yourself coming to church every Sunday and knowing that your job is to help the white man preserve an ungodly status quo.

JONATHAN: Remember Masechaba that I'm doing a job like any other person who wakes up in the morning to go to work for a white man in town. On Friday when that person gets his salary I also get my salary.

MASECHABA: But the difference is that your salary is dirty. It is enveloped with the blood of your own brothers!

BOTH [*responding loudly to the priest at the altar*]: Amen!

Different hymn, softer. MASECHABA *rises to go to the front to receive the sacrament. As she kneels,* JONATHAN *follows her and kneels beside her. She opens her mouth.*

MASECHABA: Amen! [*Crosses herself*]

JONATHAN [*receives the communion*]: Amen!

She goes back to her previous position. A little later he follows. Then he challenges her as the hymn goes softer.

JONATHAN: How many children die of malnutrition because their parents cannot find jobs? I have mouths to feed. [*Makes sure he is not heard by other congregants.*] I have my children's school fees to attend to. Do you know that since I took up this job things have changed for the better for me. I'm also convinced that we must stand aloof from politics. We are servants of God and God does not wish us to enter the political arena.

MASECHABA: I've had enough of this senseless talk. The sermon delivered by the priest is enough. I'm not going to listen to a sell-out sermon from you Jonathan, you are a bloodsucker. You have no conscience. You are dead inside.

JONATHAN: What do you mean I'm dead? I'm alive. I've the same feelings as you.

MASECHABA [*shifting away from him slightly*]: I knew you wouldn't understand me.

By dead [*blue light comes up, simultaneously general light fades down.*]
I mean the smile you put on when the enemy grins at you.
Death is when the colour of your skin turns against you and you don't
know where you stand as others decide your fate.
Death is the smile you put on when the enemy grins at you.
Death is when you stop being you! And above all,

[*General lights come up whilst the blue fades down.*]

Death, is when you start to hate to be black!

A closing hymn.

JONATHAN: Masechaba you are too hasty to condemn me before you understand my situation better. Maybe we are not so different after all.

MASECHABA: Ag fuck off you are a sellout! [*She moves away.*]

JONATHAN [*humiliated and disregarding the congregants*]: Hey Masechaba
you ridicule me in the presence of all these people – that is nice for you.
[MASECHABA *heads for the door and he calls after her*]

But one day you'll know who I am. Then you'll know what death is.
Mcundu wakho! Lentombi iyandigezela, masemb'akho! Shit! Bastard! [*Re-
alises the Bible is still in his hand. Quickly crosses himself as he exits.*]
Oh! I'm sorry Lord!

Blackout

Second Encounter

WHITEBEARD *is sorting out some documents at the table.*

WHITEBEARD: Jonathan, where are those poems of Masechaba's that the Soweto Business Association is complaining about?

JONATHAN: Which ones are those sir?

WHITEBEARD: The ones I gave you to photostat.

JONATHAN [*to himself as he goes through his bag*]: My driver's licence, my insurance contract. O sir look, my daughter turned two years yesterday, this is her picture taken last night.

WHITEBEARD [*businesslike*]: Later Jonathan. Bring me the poems. [*Jonathan gives him the poems.*]
  Now call the poet inside.

JONATHAN [*opens the door and calls out*]: Masechaba!

She walks in and stops. JONATHAN *stands at the door.*

WHITEBEARD: Miss Masechaba, you disappoint me. When I had you in here the last time I thought we'd come to some understanding. But when I read these poems I'm not sure. Sit down please, and listen objectively to these poems of yours. I'm going to read them the way you do . . .

MASECHABA: No. If they have to be read I'll read them for you, I wrote them.

WHITEBEARD: No! I want you to hear the way they sound.

[MASECHABA *stands to take the page from* WHITEBEARD *but* JONATHAN *quickly steps in and looks at her threateningly.* MASECHABA *stops, realises the risk and sits down.* JONATHAN *walks back to his previous position.* WHITEBEARD *starts to read the poem out loud with agitation.*]

  Look deep into the ghetto

And see the modernised graves,
Where only the living-dead exist
Manacled with chains
So as not to resist.
Look deep into the ghetto
And see streets dividing the graves
Streets with pavements
Dyed with blood
Blood of the innocent.
Look deep into the ghetto
And see yourself silenced
By a ninety-nine year lease
Thus creating a class struggle
Within a struggle for survival
Look the ghetto over
You will see smog hover
And dust choking the lifeless living dead
Can you hear the beasts hell
And creatures evil
Howling and brawling
As they rush to devour you
and suck the last drop of blood
From your emaciated corpse . . .

MASECHABA: That is not the way the poem is . . .

WHITEBEARD: I haven't finished yet. [*Pause.*] Now, 'class struggle', that is Marxist talk. It is dangerous talk Miss Masechaba. Don't you feel that Marxism and Africanism are contradictory?

MASECHABA: No. They are not contradictory.

WHITEBEARD: Oh! So you admit that you are a Marxist.

MASECHABA: I didn't say that.

WHITEBEARD: I'm glad you didn't say that. Because if you had you wouldn't be here with me. Miss Masechaba you're fortunate that you're here with me tonight because some of my colleagues would have dealt with you firmly.

[*Slight pause.*]

You puzzle me Miss Masechaba. You claim to be an Africanist and yet when one of your people goes out to improve his or her living conditions and when some of them participate in the political organs made available to them you attack them.

Can't you see that places like Crossroads and Mogopa are a health hazard? Can't you see that the proliferation of shacks and shanties in the townships are a drawback to those blacks who want to live a better life? What is your Black Consciousness motto? 'Black man you are on your own.' Why then do you try and belittle the black men who are trying to go on their own by owning businesses and improving their living conditions? It seems you in your poetry attack them.

MASECHABA: You have spoken about two groups of people. Besides you know that I am not attacking those who are caught in the capitalists' spider's web . . .

WHITEBEARD: Who do you attack then? You go about attacking your own people and then you tell me there are two groups. I want you to tell me here and now who your attack is aimed at? [*No response.*]

I asked you a question. Who do you attack?

General lights fade, blue comes up.
MASECHABA [*standing on a chair*]:

> On the wings of the storm of liberation
> Waving black tickets in their hands
> Degrees hanging like monuments of heroes
> In their glass houses
> Sit the cheese and wine drinkers
> Of our struggle.
>
> Others are undegreed
> Unread, underpaid
> And deprived of the right to quench
> Their education thirst.
> Pity, they too are caught in the web.
>
> The motto reads thus!
> 'Divide and rule'
> A new dispensation
> Is the name of the game.
> The ghetto is fast becoming a suburb
> Beverley Hills
> Selection Park
> Prestige Park
> Monument Park

'Who cares
'It's my sweat
'It's my money
'You're just wasting your time
'Damn it. I'm going out
'To have a swim.'

Hats off for the Master's plan!
We salute you Soweto Homemakers' Festival!
Thank you Urban Foundation!
Thank you Gough Cooper!
Thank you Mr Constructive Engagement!
Thank you 'Iron Lady'
Voetsek! You have messed up our struggle!

General lights come up, blue light fades.

WHITEBEARD: I asked you a question – who do you attack?

MASECHABA [*seemingly inattentive and still seated*]:   The cheese and wine drinkers of our struggle.

WHITEBEARD: Always a poet. That rings a bell – here in this poem you write 'silenced by a ninety-nine year lease . . . Selection Park, Monument Park . . .' It seems to me Miss Masechaba that these people who go and live in these better suburbs are worthy of your contempt?

MASECHABA: Everything I feel is in the poem and the poem says it all . . .

WHITEBEARD: Would I be correct in assuming that organisations like for example the Soweto Business Association are targets of your attack?

MASECHABA: You can make up your mind on that.

WHITEBEARD [*tension as their eyes lock. Pause*]:   I'll do that! You may go. [*Before* MASECHABA *reaches the door.*]
    One more thing before you go. [MASECHABA *stops.*] It might interest you Miss Masechaba, to know that a lot of people give us information. Normally we don't want to share it but sometimes we do. Every Thursday night for the past four weeks you've been going to these rent boycott meetings and reciting your poetry in support of those leaders of yours who've been saying to the people 'Don't go and live in Selection Park, don't go to that petit-bourgeois place'. It might interest you to know that those very same people have applied for bigger and better houses in Beverley Hills and Prestige Park. Would you like to see their names? [*He tries to pass a book to her. She is not interested.*]

93

I thought not. What about those Black Consciousness, Afrika for the Africans leaders of yours who send their children secretly to white schools to get a white education – would you like to see their names?

MASECHABA: Every struggle has its betrayers. My leader is the people.

WHITEBEARD: The people? [*Disappointed.*] I'll try and remember that. [*Gestures with finger to dismiss her and then remembers something. This action is intended deliberately to torment her.*]

Oh, just before you go, I have a poem of yours which seems to be written in some ethnic language. Would you tell me what it means? It's called Hoy, Hoy, Hoy-in-a-Hoyini . . .

General light fades. Blue light comes up.

MASECHABA:

Hoyina!!
Nivile nga maculo
Esizwe sintsundu e-Azania
Ethetha ngokuthi asifikanga apha
We have no history of arrival
Kuya mangalisa
Asihlalanga ngoxolo ezweni lethu
Simile kodwa ngomlenz'omnye
Siphandliwe simana siyalila
Sovuthelwa ngubanina
Namhlanje siyagxothwa
Ngomso siyabotshwa
Hayi ngenyimini siyazilwela
We fight back
Unzima lomthwalo womzabalazo

Abanye bayathengisa
Abanye bayathengiswa
Kuvuthumlilo
Ithayela lityumtu
Kwenze njanina sizwe' sintsundu
Aqhubeka njalo
Amaculo esizwe sintsundu e-Azania
Igcwele imigaqo ngabasebenzi
Bayazabalaza nabo
Baqhubeka phambili

94

Abantwana bayalishukumisa ilizwe
Baculela phezulu
Bazama ngapha nangapha
Bayalinyikimisa
Bayalizongomisa
Ngomso ngenene sophumelela

Abasetyhini bayalilizela
Sengathi kumnandi kowethu
Kanti thina siyazi
It is the African
Way of doing things
Even the revolution!

Blue light fades, general light comes up.

WHITEBEARD: It's called 'Hoyina'. Would you care to tell me what it means?

MASECHABA [*immediately*]:   No! I'm sure you have translators in here who would be happy to do it for you.

She walks out angrily. As she pulls the door open, she's pushed back into the room by JONATHAN *who's been standing outside the door. He walks a few steps towards her as she steps backwards.*

WHITEBEARD [*angrily*]:   Masechaba. [*Points to a chair.* MASECHABA *sits down.*]

Jonathan, it seems you are going to get a chance to read this after all. [*Hands him a written page.*] Read clauses four, five and six out loud.

JONATHAN: Clause Four: You are to report at your nearest police station daily before eight o'clock every evening. Clause Five: You are not to attend any gathering and note that talking to more than one person at a time will be a contravention of your banning order. Clause six: This banning order is imposed on you for the next three years.

WHITEBEARD: I warned you, and you chose to ignore my friendly advice. You asked for it. Jonathan explain the full implications of that document to our Soweto poet laureate.

He makes a move for the door.

MASECHABA [*standing*]:   Just before you go, Major! [WHITEBEARD *returns and stands in front of her. He is obviously shocked at her nerve in calling him back as he called her back. There is more tension as she addresses him.*] Mr William Shakespeare wrote some very wonderful lines about you which go:

95

Man proud man,
Dressed in a little brief authority
Plays such fantastic tricks before high heaven
As makes the angels weep.

WHITEBEARD [*chuckling*]: You really amuse me. What did you expect me to answer? Who is this Shakespeare? What political organisation does he belong to? [*Softer, but hard.*] We are not as stupid as you might think. [*He leaves.* MASECHABA *sits down. She is obviously shattered by the banning order.*]

JONATHAN: Ya Masechaba, poet of the people! Where are all the people you were preaching poetry to? Do you think the people will eat your poetry when they starve?. Let me tell you something. I can't be led by a bastard like you! I know your kind. Showing off all the time with your name on the front pages of newspapers. All you know is jet-setting from time to time, and then you think you can fool us with your petty politics. Ha! You think we are impressed by your behaviour in your two-piece costumes – carrying an executive bag when you go and talk to the same white people that you criticise. Ah! but when you read your poetry you put on African dresses, use revolutionary language and then you think you can fool everybody. [*Laughs.*] Bigmouth, I'm talking to you. Talk! You've just earned yourself a banning order!

MASECHABA [*grabs the banning order, crumples it and throws it away*]: This is just a piece of paper – I'm still myself. My conscience is clear . . . The people out there are waiting for me – Masechaba, Mother of the Nation . . . That's what the name means if you don't know. If they have to wait for you, it will only be to tear you apart! They will scorn you, they'll reject you!

JONATHAN: C'mon enjoy yourself for this is your last poetry session . . .

MASECHABA: Yes, they can ban me here but they won't ban the spirit of the nation. For as long as those millions of people are still thirsty the march will continue. I respect the convictions of my people and they respect my beliefs. I will help them carry the cross . . .

JONATHAN: Don't give me this shit about 'your people'. I know your kind . . .

MASECHABA: You don't know for you have no conscience.

JONATHAN: It's easy for you because you get your money from the World Council of Churches. You have nothing to lose, because you have no mouths to feed . . .

96

MASECHABA: And so that is what makes you sell your people out? Why don't you stand up and pull up your pants and tell the white man it's enough – your face against his; tell him you've had enough . . .

JONATHAN: You are dreaming, for the white man is in power – can't you see?

MASECHABA [*changes mood*]: Jonathan, you don't understand. You are black and I'm black . . .

JONATHAN: And then?

MASECHABA: In the beginning it was you and me. The land belonged to us. We tilled it. We shared everything equally. Then came the white man with his own thoughts. He put us asunder; put us against each other and while this was going on, he fenced us around and then moved about freely declaring our land his land – no man's land. Did you not seen those boards along the road as you came from home this morning, saying: 'In front of you, behind you and all around you is a Rand Mines Property?' Have you bothered to ask yourself 'where did Rand Mines get our land from? Who did he buy it from? He took it with the gun. Do you know what the white man is doing today? He is sharing every little bit of our soil equally with his own brother. [JONATHAN *is torn apart.*]

The system is so planned that we don't realise these tricks easily. [*Her voice builds up.*] Why should we let the white man decide our fate? Are we not matured to know and understand the world around us? [*She hoists his hand and fits her palm into his.*] The white man is aware that your clenched fist together with mine is the dawning of a new era. And when that dawn comes, no amount of machinery will put us apart. This is the spirit of the nation! And this is what moves the people today!

WHITEBEARD [*bursting in*]: Masechaba! [JONATHAN *pulls his hand away and stands a distance away from her.*] You have overstayed your welcome! [*Picks up the crumpled banning order and puts it into Masechaba's pocket.* MASECHABA *exits.*]

JONATHAN [*guilty*]: Major, what she was saying to me – there is sense in her talk . . .

WHITEBEARD: Do you think she makes sense?

JONATHAN: I . . . I . . . I think . . .

WHITEBEARD: Let me make some sense to you. How many children have you got?

JONATHAN: Four, Major.

97

WHITEBEARD: Where are they being educated?

JONATHAN: Waterford, in Swaziland.

WHITEBEARD: And who pays for their education?

JONATHAN: You do, sir, as a benefit for me.

WHITEBEARD: Am I making sense Jonathan. Am I making sense?

JONATHAN [*embarrassed*]: Yes Sir!

WHITEBEARD: Now, I'm detaching you from normal duties. I want you to organise a team of four men to follow her wherever she goes. I want to know who she meets. I want her telephone tapped and mail screened. I have a suspicion that since the bastard is banned she is going to pursue her activities underground. I want you to do a good job... Hear me Jonathan?

JONATHAN: Yes sir. [*Slight pause.*] By the way Major, you promised that I could take the blue Mercedes Benz home for the weekend.

WHITEBEARD: Yes. The keys are in the key-box.

JONATHAN [*excited*]: Thank you sir!

Blackout

[*Back in the township* MASECHABA *continues to read her poetry in public, defying the banning order. The following poem can be read from any part of the stage as long as the position will not confuse the location. Blue light comes on.*]

MASECHABA:

Apartheid!
You maintained yourself
By keeping us separate
You were father of many
Like Suppression of Communism Act

Who killed many
Who hanged many
Who maimed many

And when later you realised
He was not doing you good
You killed him

Amongst your sons
Bantu Education

98

Stripped many
Of their brains

Made them docile
Killed many
Maimed many
Jailed many

And now you realise
He is not doing you good
You want to kill him
I remember your other son
Old and notorious
Pass-Law
Never smiled
Just locked millions
And I heard yesterday
He died
And millions are beginning to smile
I hope he is not resurrected underground
As for you
I heard your bodyguard Botha say
You are outdated
And wants to send you to the grave
But he defended you
By sending many of us to their graves

I think we must bring him to trial
Like all Nazi war criminals
How's that?

Blue light fades.

Third Encounter

MASECHABA is arrested. Special light comes up on MASECHABA's face behind bars. She is dressed in her nightgown and her feet are bare. This part can also be depicted by light – no specific stage area.

MASECHABA:

> They broke one window first
> Then on all windows played sounds
> Made by the drums of wars
> Both doors joined the chorus
> The front emitting quick soprano notes
> The back a slow dub-dub-dub
>
> It all happened in minutes
> The vocalists shouted
> The notes one after the other
> Like they'd never rehearsed before
> Vula! Vula! Bulang man!
> Open up! The lyrics went
> The timing was bad.
>
> This is the music
> That has become notorious
> It plays at the first hour of the day
> When your name rings
> To be registered in the books
> Of those messengers of darkness
> You jump to your feet
>
> Try to say something you think makes sense
> You take all your poems

Hide all manuscripts
Throw some into the stove
To destroy the creation
rather than see it defiled by them
With their dirty hands.

If you are the poet's sister
'Don't open they are thugs!'
And then the poet will follow
'We won't open you are thugs!'
To give herself time to destroy
Everything and quickly relay messages
To the family.

But then the door has to be opened
Delaying tactics won't last forever
You saw it in Zimbabwe
The back door is kicked open
While you open the front
Within seconds

The musicians spit their songs into every room
While others guard the doors for escapers.
Torches flashing all over!
And the poet is taken.

Jonathan comes to take her out of the cell and pushes her into the interrogation room. She falls on her knees.

MASECHABA [*exhausted and still handcuffed*]:   I could not say no to them. Does the impala say no to the lion? Could the Star of David say no to the jackboot? I could not say no.

[JONATHAN *walks behind her.* WHITEBEARD *bursts in. He switches on the tape. Tension.* MASECHABA *stands up to challenge him.*]

And why do all this to me . . .

WHITEBEARD: Shut up! If I want you to talk I'll order you! Miss Masechaba, spirit of the nation, poet, word merchant, what is the protector of the state? [*No response*] I asked you a question. What is the protector of the state? Jonathan, will you tell Miss Masechaba what the protector of the state is?

JONATHAN: Yes. The law.

WHITEBEARD: And you Miss Masechaba have chosen to break that law . . .

MASECHABA: I have not . . .

WHITEBEARD: Shut up! Six months ago I had you in my office, I talked to you person-to-person. One intelligence to what I thought was another intelligence. I said to you Miss Masechaba, your poetry is inciting the people. Please, I said to you, you are a woman of reason, stop this! You are treading on a dangerous path. You wouldn't listen to me. Three months later, I bring you in here again. I say to you, I'm sorry, justice has to prevail everywhere. I don't want to do this to you, I respect you, but the law has decided, here is your banning order for your own protection. That too is not good enough for Miss Masechaba . . .

MASECHABA: But . . .

WHITEBEARD: Shut up! Miss Masechaba has to ignore the provisions of her banning order. She has to go out into the halls and she has to say to the people, 'you see my banning order. This is what I do to my banning order!' [*He raises his hand and shows his palm to the audience. He spits on it.*] I could live with that Miss Masechaba, I could just live with it. But then yesterday something happened. I have a press release which is going out this afternoon . . . [*First he goes to wipe his hand on her shoulder, then goes to his table, produces a document and reads it out to her.*]

'Yesterday evening patrol police spotted four men who they suspected were part of the fifty cadres that crossed the border into the country and when the terrorists realised they were being followed they opened fire on the police who responded by killing all four men. None of the police was injured. Large quantities of arms and ammunition and literature were captured.'

Now Miss Masechaba, amongst the AK47s, Scorpions and limpet mines; among the T5s and T7s; amongst those instruments of terror that were going to sow discord and violence among your people as well as mine, among them was a book of your poetry with the inscription inside [*He produces the book.*] 'To LMA – solidarity and strength my comrades – Masechaba'.

MASECHABA: I have signed lots of autographs in my poetry books. When people bring them to me to sign what do I do? Do I refuse? As for LMA, I don't know who he is . . .

WHITEBEARD: Who is LMA?

MASECHABA: I said I do not know.

WHITEBEARD [*going closer to her and punching her in the stomach*]: I asked you a question. Who is LMA?

102

MASECHABA [*writhing in pain*]:   How must I talk to convince you that I do not know? Are you ever going to understand my language?

WHITEBEARD [*making as if to punch her again*]:   I have no desire to understand your language. [*Sarcastic assurance.*] You don't need to be scared of me, remember we are friends. [*He rushes to the table.*] I have a confession to make to a friend. Yes, Miss Masechaba, you have been followed night and day. Yes you have been watched [*indicating from a list in his hands*]. This is a known terrorist hideout, that is a known terrorist hideout. That is a shebeen where terrorists are known to congregate. Is it coincidence that you visited these places on your poetic pilgrimage? What organisation do you belong to?

MASECHABA: I do not belong to any organisation.

WHITEBEARD: Isn't the African Poets of Azania an organisation? Is that not an organisation?

MASECHABA: It is a cultural body. It's a traditional African ensemble . . .

WHITEBEARD: Is it not an organisation?

MASECHABA: Yes it is.

WHITEBEARD: Are you not their member?

MASECHABA: Yes I am.

WHITEBEARD *presses the tape to play back* MASECHABA's *denials: 'I do not belong to any organisation'.*

WHITEBEARD: Now you tell me you do. Do you know what that means Miss Masechaba? That means my friend that you are lying to me and I don't like that. You've just told me one lie, how do I know how many other lies you have told me? I think I must give you a chance to decide whether you want to continue lying to me. [*He pulls her by the handcuffs.*] Jonathan, will you teach Miss Masechaba what we do to people who tell lies. [*Walks out.*]

JONATHAN *takes out a rope and hooks it to the handcuffed hands and then orders her to squat while he relaxes. This continues until he falls asleep. The lights fade to a blackout. She continues to squat until she falls down. Lights come up.*

WHITEBEARD *comes back.* JONATHAN *jumps to his feet.*

WHITEBEARD: Poor Miss Masechaba has been treated so badly. Jonathan, what have you done? [JONATHAN *does not respond. He knows* WHITEBEARD's *tricks during interrogations.* WHITEBEARD *changes moods.*]

103

Weren't you taught manners, kaffir, that when you're in the presence of the white man you must stand up? [*He kicks her.*] Up! Up! I can't talk to a grown woman on the floor. Up! [MASECHABA *stands.*] Who is LMA?

MASECHABA: I said I do not know.

WHITEBEARD [*taking some documents from the drawers of his table*]: These are all the names and addresses of people you communicated with regularly – have you anything to say?

MASECHABA: I have communicated with lots of friends in the past, some of them are fellow writers. Do you expect me to live in isolation? I'm human.

WHITEBEARD: There you are, agreeing that you have something in common with the people on our lists.

MASECHABA: Whatever my friends do because of their convictions has nothing to do with me. I'm a simple poet.

WHITEBEARD: Yes, a poet you are, but I don't think you are that simple. I have here photographs of two of your best friends who've skipped the country and received training in Moscow and in Africa. How do you respond to your friends doing that?

MASECHABA: Your government sells diamonds to Moscow. It is known to be geting arms from Bulgaria. How do you respond to your friends doing that?

WHITEBEARD: Did you hear that Jonathan? Our poet friend fancies herself as a foreign policy analyst. Now you listen very carefully. You see these hands. They are clean, unsoiled and they look friendly. Every day when these hands get home, they lift up a one-year-old bundle called David and they throw him into the air and they catch him, they tickle him and hold him steady as he threatens to fall over with pure enjoyment. But Miss Masechaba, in order to protect that little boy from you and your Marxist friends, to stop your violence and terror from changing that little boy's joy to tears, these hands will do anything, [*hits her with both hands*], anything! And the blood will wash off very easily. Do you understand me? I asked you a question. Do you understand me? Well my friend, seeing that you don't understand my words maybe you'll understand my actions [*He throttles her and throws her to the floor. MASECHABA falls and writhes in pain. He kicks her in the stomach. Pause.*] Is there anything that you don't understand?

MASECHABA [*on her knees boldly faces* WHITEBEARD]: So deep is my love for my land that those who fail to understand seek to destroy me.

[*She stands up slowly.*]

> Perhaps, finally at the very end
> When the curtain falls
> On the last act of your pillage
> You will come to understand
> How deeply
> We loved this land
> And cared for all its people

[*Upright and facing forward.*]

> White and black
> Free and unfree

There is silence and tension.

WHITEBEARD: Jonathan, will you deal with Masechaba as you deem fit and if you have to teach her that electricity has other uses than providing light you must do it!

JONATHAN [*in a dilemma*]: But sir, it seems from the look of things she does not know who this LMA is. Besides, she's an ordinary poet.

WHITEBEARD [*angrily*]: Do I have to start wondering where your loyalties lie Jonathan?

JONATHAN: No sir!

WHITEBEARD: Then do it! [WHITEBEARD *exits leaving the two behind. A little later Jonathan takes off his jacket to start the torture of* MASECHABA *as lights fade to blackout*]

Fourth Encounter

Lights come up instantly on the cell area. MASECHABA's *body is lying on a slab covered with a blanket. A hood covers her head.* WHITEBEARD *stands to the left of the slab with* JONATHAN *opposite him. The atmosphere is tense.* JONATHAN *puts on his jacket.* WHITEBEARD *begins to walk nervously round the slab.* JONATHAN *does the same to make way for* WHITEBEARD.

WHITEBEARD: So, this is what you did?

JONATHAN: Yes my lord.

WHITEBEARD: How long has she been like this?

JONATHAN: My lord knows.

WHITEBEARD: I forget!

JONATHAN: One week!

WHITEBEARD: So, so! [*Pause.*] This is serious! I'll have to see what I can do. Why the slab?

JONATHAN: So that you can see her well!

WHITEBEARD: Why the blanket?

JONATHAN: To have her covered!

WHITEBEARD: Why the hood?

JONATHAN: To help hide the head!

WHITEBEARD: What?

JONATHAN: It is common practice my lord that when detainees are in this state, we cover their heads.

WHITEBEARD: It is a stupid procedure to have them covered all the time! She was healthier when I last saw her!

Blackout.

Fifth Encounter

In the cell a few hours later. The slab is positioned in a different place.
WHITEBEARD *and* JONATHAN *walk round it.*

WHITEBEARD: How's the head?

JONATHAN: As before.

WHITEBEAD: I forget! [JONATHAN *moves towards* MASECHABA *to show her head.*]

      Say it! [JONATHAN *stops.*]

JONATHAN: Septic.

WHITEBEARD: Colour?

JONATHAN: Red and pink.

WHITEBEARD: Put calamine lotion on head.

JONATHAN: Okay my lord. I make a note. Calamine lotion on head.

[He takes out pad and pencil and makes notes. A piece of rope protrudes from his pocket.]

WHITEBEARD: And why the rope?

JONATHAN: Used during interrogation.

WHITEBEARD: Unnecessary evidence!

JONATHAN: I make a note.

      [*Writes again.*] Rope to discard. [*Slowly, with a sad look on his face.*] Rope to discard.

WHITEBEARD: What is wrong now Jonathan?

JONATHAN: I remember seeing her hands many times in church.

WHITEBEARD: Remember, you had a job to do.

JONATHAN: Yes my lord.

107

Sixth Encounter

In the cell a few hours later. The slab has been removed. MASECHABA's *body lies sprawled on the floor.*

WHITEBEARD: What will you tell the court?

JONATHAN: I'll say she threw herself out of the window in an attempt to escape . . .

WHITEBEARD: No good. The interrogation room is on the ground floor!

JONATHAN: No, no, it's simple. We called her in to have breakfast with us – she was so hungry that she ate her food so fast that it choked her . . .

WHITEBEARD: Not convincing. We never have breakfast with detainees in our rooms.

JONATHAN [*tries again*]: All right, I'll say she was on a hunger strike since we took her in.

WHITEBEARD: No! Jonathan when last did you check your record books? We gave that excuse some time ago!

JONATHAN [*still panicking*]: How about saying she hanged herself with her gown-strap, that's right! [*exited*] Suicide!

WHITEBEARD: Not convincing. There's nothing in the cell to hang herself from!

JONATHAN [*a bit hopeless but tries . . . to himself*]: Seems like nothing is convincing. I'll try one more time . . . [*hilarious with excitement*] She slipped on a piece of soap . . . !

WHITEBEARD: You can't fool the public with that one again!

JONATHAN [*defeated*]: My lord knows all . . .

WHITEBEARD: Maybe we should look back at our history with her. Maybe that will give us a clue.

JONATHAN: Yes my lord. Maybe that will give us an idea. [JONATHAN *exits.*] *Blackout.*

Seventh Encounter

In the cell one day later. WHITEBEARD *and* JONATHAN *are among huge piles of files.* MASECHABA's *body is in the same position as before.* JONATHAN *drops the files on the floor one after the other.*

JONATHAN [*apologetic*]: Some pages are missing sir . . .

WHITEBEARD [*authoritative*]: Confidential to The Party!

A pause as JONATHAN *continues his search through the files.*

JONATHAN: When will the pathologist see her sir?

WHITEBEARD: That too is confidential to The Party. Be here on Sunday. Eight o'clock. Write your statement in full.

JONATHAN: Should I make up anything?

WHITEBEARD: No! That's important. He has to know what direction to channel his finding. Let him know it. What happened. Where. When it happened and who was present.

JONATHAN: I'll remember. I make a note. [*Louder.*] Details of torture in full . . .!

WHITEBEARD: Shhh! Walls have ears. I pray they don't have a private pathologist.

JONATHAN: Will you allow it sir . . .?

WHITEBEARD: Sometimes we have to show off our democratic processes. Now let's take a closer look at her.

JONATHAN: Why my lord?

WHITEBEARD: Don't be stupid we must make our own study.

JONATHAN: Fine. Orders taken.

WHITEBEARD: Remove the hood, the blanket. [JONATHAN *is slow.*] Snap to it! I have a meeting with the pathologist!

JONATHAN: Like to see her naked?

WHITEBEARD [*irritated*]: Quick! The court will order it. This looks horrible
– cover her up!
   [*JONATHAN covers the body*] Calamine all visible wounds.

WHITEBEARD: The gown, why did you do it when she had it on?

JONATHAN: She refused to change into different clothes when I ordered her
to.

Another long pause

WHITEBEARD: Now bring back the slab. Move it to the right. [JONATHAN
does as instructed.] More. Pick up the body and put it back on the slab.
Higher. Make sure that we see all parts of her body before we make the
first press statements.

JONATHAN: Why my lord?

WHITEBEARD: Don't be stupid, the family may order a public enquiry!

JONATHAN: Fine. Orders taken.

WHITEBEARD: Remove the blanket again. Bare the chest. [JONATHAN *un-
buttons the gown and steps back.*] Now let's go to the legs. [*He rolls the
gown up.*] Higher. Put calamine on chest and legs.

JONATHAN: I make a note. Calamine chest and legs.

WHITEBEARD *and* JONATHAN *take a final look at* MASECHABA *as in the
opening scene.*

JONATHAN: What if we were to clothe her in prison attire?

WHITEBEARD: That's stupid! This is detention. She hasn't been to prison yet.

JONATHAN [*humiliated*]: My lord knows everything.

More contemplation of MASECHABA.

WHITEBEARD: That's enough for the day and remember whatever happens
DON'T PANIC! You've proved your loyalty and I'll do everything to protect you!

He puts his arm around JONATHAN *as they walk away and freeze at some
point with their faces looking down as if shying away from the public eye.*

   General lights fade as Special comes up on MASECHABA's *head and shoulders.
Slow fade to semi-darkness on* WHITEBEARD *and* JONATHAN *so that their
shadows can be seen.* MASECHABA's *voice can be heard reciting her last poem*

110

Epilogue (*on tape*)

When the parricidal mania
That grips the uncrowned villains
Roams free
And the streets are
Dyed with blood
They would seek me out to pray together
At the altar
For they would have come to realise
That I was against their own destruction
And clung frantically
On the frail hope
That they would be brought to sanity

Perhaps finally
They would be calling me out
To rebuke the storms
But all hope and understanding
Shall have gone by then

Slow fade both positions to blackout.

Ndizimisele Bhedesho, Mthuthuzeli Sozwe

JIKA

Jika was first performed at the Workshop Theatre at the University of Leeds, UK, in 1986 by Mthuthuzeli Sozwe and Ndizimisele Bedesho from Uitenhage and then at the New Federal Theatre in New York in 1988 featuring Jerry Mathibe Mofokeng and Fana Kekana.

In 1991 it was performed in South Africa by Makwela Lekalakala and Vusi Kunene of the School of Dramatic Art, University of the Witwatersrand, Johannesburg.

All productions were directed by Maishe Maponya.

With much gratitude to the Workshop Theatre, Leeds, New Federal Theatre, New York and the School of Dramatic Art, Johannesburg.

SETTING: The performance is set against a background of 4 x 4 m scaffolding erected 1½ m from the cyclorama or back wall facing the audience. The reader must be very imaginative as the scaffolding will be used for various settings. It is not compulsory to use scaffolding, a flat 3 x 3 m will do. When used, the scaffolding in the first scene will be a school yard fence. In the hostel scenes, the area behind the scaffolding should be seen as a township and a road along which the characters will walk on their long journey from the village hideout. It also serves as a prison when the two comrades are finally arrested by the police during a dawn raid on the hostel where they have lived for months. Two rostra of the same dimensions covering an area 1 m in depth, 3 m in length and 12 cm in height should be placed alongside each other in the front and back of the scaffolding. On both wings of the stage there are flats which the actors will use from time to time for costume changes.

Scene One

The play opens in a school yard where hundreds of students have gathered. It is morning and as is traditional before any gathering, they sing, waving their fists in the air, and circle around the school yard. Outside the school yard, the police in 'hippos' and army trucks 'observe' the event, keen-eyed and probably in disgust. The students disregard them and sing:

STUDENTS:

Hei Botha	Botha
Usithatha Kanjani	How dare you
Ubulalisa isizwe	undermine our people
Wena Botha	by (letting your army
usithatha kanjani	and police) kill
Ubulalisa isizwe	our people
sizo Bulala	We will
Thina Sobulala' Mabhunu . . .	Kill the Boers . . .

The song continues as FIRST STUDENT *climbs the fence (scaffolding) and calls for silence before addressing the students.*

FIRST STUDENT: Now, comrades, these leaflets dropped in the morning by our 'friends' now surrounding us outside the fence, do not attempt to solve the schools' problems we have faced for years nor do they show any indication towards a better life for all the inhabitants of our country. You see comrades, the whole issue now lies in our hands, not in the hands of the school teachers who have been conditioned and intimidated to understand this ridiculous leaflet. I do not suggest that all our school teachers have sold us out – no! We want our own freely elected student leaders drawn from all over the country. A ga go bjalo comrades (Is that not so comrades)? Yes. The new education system must be planned and structured by our own educationists elected by us not those who have oppressed our people for centuries.

115

The claims of this document that there are instigators amongst the students are false. If there are any instigators, it is the government – they must be the ones banished for life for the evils and irreparable damage they have done to our people ...

Enter the PRINCIPAL *shouting from a distance.*

PRINCIPAL: Ehhh Children! Listen. Your grievances are now being sorted out by the authorities. Meanwhile, you are ordered to leave these premises until a final decision has been made ...

FIRST STUDENT: Bjalo gona comrades ba a re gafela ... that is madness comrades ...

PRINCIPAL [*continues talking*] : ... You will be informed about the procedure and details of when to return. Lastly, you are requested not to walk in numbers exceeding three when you are outside the school premises! Is that clear?

FIRST STUDENT: With all due respect, sir, we are all very sorry to say that we are here by the will of all students of this school. We are not prepared to leave until our demands are met! And remember our major demand, allow us to form a freely elected Student Representative Council.

The PRINCIPAL *calls* FIRST STUDENT *aside and can be seen gesticulating in a pleading manner.*

PRINCIPAL: Tokologo! Tokologo my son come here.

FIRST STUDENT [*moving away from him*]: Don't ask me to announce anything to the students.

PRINCIPAL: Well, well ... if you feel so strong about your position there's not much I can do ... You know how limited my powers are. Please! I do not want you to be hurt ...

There is a distant sound of approaching army trucks.

FIRST STUDENT: Oh God – listen comrades, the police have been called in. We must not panic. We must stand here and sing. No one is allowed to provoke them and no stone throwing. Is that clear?

They start to sing.

STUDENTS: Soze sisuswe ngamabhulu ezweni Iokhokho bethu... [*repeat*] (We will not be moved by the boers in the land of our forefathers...)

THE POLICE [*through a loudspeaker*]: Aandag! Aandag! Attention! This is Sergeant Koekemoer speaking. You do not want to listen to the principal?

All right, no matter what you think, we are here to restore order! Now listen to me . . . You are given two minutes, only two minutes to disperse!

FIRST STUDENT: He's mad comrades, we are going nowhere!

The singing continues as the police storm the school yard with dogs and guns. The students stumble and choke with teargas.

SECOND STUDENT: My eyes are burning! Help me someone please . . . give me some water . . . Oh God. [*He sees an injured boy on the ground*] Look at this young boy [*tries to talk to him*]. Tell me, what is your name? C'mon speak to me. I want to help you . . . Oh God, he's dead. But why did you let it happen Lord, why?

FIRST STUDENT *approaches*

FIRST STUDENT: Mayibuye, is that one also dead?

SECOND STUDENT: Yes. He's just died in my hands . . .

FIRST STUDENT: Oh no my friend someone has to speak to the gods.

SECOND STUDENT [*kneeling beside the boy*]: Strange gods of the heavens. We stand beneath this shadow of death; and so do innocent men, women and children. We plead, we plead for the lives of our people who have been enslaved for many years. Please, strange gods, have mercy . . . [*A bullet whizzes past and they duck.*] What's that?

FIRST STUDENT: It's the sound of a gun.

SECOND STUDENT: Come let's run away. That way . . . [*pulls him by the hand, they run and stop.*]

FIRST STUDENT [*talking softly*]: Can you hear the dogs barking? Come, this way . . .

SECOND STUDENT: Yes. [*They run and stop, crouching.*] The whole place is sealed. Look, there's an army truck approaching . . . let's pretend we are dead . . . [*They lie still for a moment.*]

FIRST STUDENT [*a little later*]: Comrade, come let's go. Comrade. [*No response.*] Comrade are you dead?

SECOND STUDENT: Hayi man!

FIRST STUDENT [*Putting his finger to his mouth*]: Shh! They are gone.

SECOND STUDENT: Let's go, that way. [*They run and stop.*] My friend, the bloody dogs are following our tracks.

FIRST STUDENT: Come, that way. [*They run even faster and stop abruptly.*]

SECOND STUDENT: My friend we are surrounded.

More panic.

FIRST STUDENT: What shall we do?

A camera flashes and they jump. They realise they have been photographed.

SECOND STUDENT: What was that?

FIRST STUDENT: We have been completely exposed.

SECOND STUDENT: Shit!

FIRST STUDENT: Fuck!

SECOND STUDENT: My friend we've got to leave this country.

FIRST STUDENT: But my friend, where shall we go?

SECOND STUDENT: Let us go to Ciskei homeland . . . there are doctors who'll help us there I'm sure. Come let us go!

FIRST STUDENT: No my friend, those people will sell us back to our enemies. Do you want to die? No! I will never go to Ciskei.

SECOND STUDENT: Then let us go to Duduza Men's Hostel; other comrades are known to have used it as a hideout.

FIRST STUDENT: Duduza Men's Hostel?

SECOND STUDENT: Yes my friend, come let us go!

They embrace each other and face opposite directions . . .

FIRST STUDENT: O my beloved country where are you going?

SECOND STUDENT: My beloved country turn around and look at yourself.

FIRST COMRADE: Tsoga o thenyake (Wake up and find yourself)!

SECOND COMRADE: Jika uzi jonge (Turn around and look at yourself)!
Blackout.

Scene Two

TIME: Months later.

PLACE: Could be anywhere.

CHARACTERS: The same student leaders but they are now called 'comrades'.

FIRST COMRADE: After our miraculous escape from death, we were put on a wanted list by the Special Branch.

SECOND COMRADE: All borders were alerted so that we could not leave the country.

FIRST COMRADE: Our identity pictures were printed in all the newspapers and a reward was put on our heads for any information leading to our arrest.

BOTH: . . . of course we did not want to skip. Life in exile was not what we wanted.

FIRST COMRADE: Some old man in the Duduza Men's Hostel gave us some make-up to conceal our identities. So we stayed in the hostel without anybody ever suspecting that we were the two student leaders who were highly wanted by the police.

SECOND COMRADE: But . . .

FIRST COMRADE: We could not escape the watchful eye of the inquisitive priest.

SECOND COMRADE: In the hostel we were met by a postman whose name we only came to know as . . .

BOTH: Comrade . . .

SECOND COMRADE: He took us to some house in the little villages of the Northern Transvaal.

FIRST COMRADE: He opened our eyes and minds about the proletariat struggle.

SECOND COMRADE: He enriched us with the *Classics of Schools Revolution.*

FIRST COMRADE: And for the first time in our lives, we learned about co-operatives and communes as an integral part of land redistribution, agrarian reform. He taught us that there is no way we could achieve liberation and freedom without revolution. Reform, he taught us, was the most dangerous step that would accelerate the process for the creation of class within the dispossessed.

SECOND COMRADE: He taught us that among the oppressed, the school only served as an institution where the downtrodden competed with each other to get certificated; since competition eliminates the majority and encourages individualism.

BOTH: And so, when we came out of the little villages of the Northern Transvaal, we were mature, sasivuthiwe. We were the two propagandists who were to return to the hostel . . .

FIRST COMRADE: To teach the toiler the ABC of proletariat struggle.

SECOND COMRADE: And to teach the school-going the ABC of education for the oppressed.

FIRST COMRADE: Often, my comrade endangered our propaganda mission as he spoke freely to the hostel-dwellers and challenged the priest who frequented the hostel on his missionary mission.

SECOND COMRADE: True, but I would only do it when I was drunk . . .

FIRST COMRADE: You lie!

SECOND COMRADE: It's true mngani wami (my friend)!

FIRST COMRADE: O nale maaka (He is lying)!

Flashback

Five years ago. The two comrades are preparing their luggage to go on a long propaganda mission. They are disguised and look like migrant workers returning to the hostel. They hum a tune softly to themselves until they arrive at Duduza Men's Hostel.

Scene Three

TIME: Months later.

PLACE: In the hostel.

CHARACTERS: As in the previous scene.

SECOND COMRADE *is talking to the hostel inmates*

SECOND COMRADE: Hee madoda [people]! We have all heard lots of people talk about 'change'. But I think it is essential for us that whilst our country is caught up in this revolutionary turmoil, we must start to grasp the full meaning of the 'change' we talk about. Otherwise, this country is heading for a bloody civil war. I want to talk about us who have been relegated to the homelands – so called. We must think about what will happen to us – and others who chant slogans without understanding their fullest meaning. Some years ago I heard one old man talk about the formation of co-operatives. He referred to those who live in the drought-stricken rural areas, like us, by saying that we could form ourselves into . . . what did he call this thing? Eh . . . yes, irrigation co-operative schemes. What could be better than this? Because, the way he put it, we could stop coming to the mines and start industries right there in the homelands.

Imagine sweet potatoes, groundnuts, sugar cane, maize and other food crops right there where we come from. Imagine these feeding first the hungry stomachs of our children in those so-called homelands. Secondly, we could become part of an exporting co-operative right there where we were relegated to extinction. Imagine the government which you will elect being the overseer of these co-operatives and communes. Gentlemen the old man was right. Co-operatives will be the most effective and essential ingredient of the people's development.

To build a powerful People's Republic of Zanj, it is essential for everyone in the villages and elsewhere in the country to work together in order to

121

achieve your liberation. Has it not dawned on you that unequal land own-
ership as perpetuated by the present regime is counter productive and counter
revolutionary . . .? [*He stops as he hears someone singing at a distance.*]
Hostel is full of crazy people. What's that? Ubani (Who)? Umfundisi (The
priest)?

PRIEST [*now very close*]:   Let us praise the Lord! Hallelujah! Oh let us praise
the Lord! Hallelujah! Brothers and sisters, it is written in the Holy Book
that you must repent and be baptised in the name of Jesus Christ for the
remission of sins, and receive the gift of the Holy Spirit for the kingdom
of God is close at hand. Brothers and sisters, it is also written in this Holy
Book that you must love your enemy as you love thy soul . . .

SECOND COMRADE: Excuse me mfundisi, how long do we have to love our
enemies?

PRIEST [*surprised*]:   What do you mean?

SECOND COMRADE: I mean mfundisi, we have been praying for a long time
and there's no answer. Now tell me how long do we have to pray?

PRIEST: My son listen to me. I'm a man of God and I trust God because
God does marvellous things. Oh my friend, [*continues to preach*] can a
man be greater than God? Look at the sky! Look at the stars, look at the
moon, God does them all. He gives us the sun, he gives us the rain, he
makes our food grow. My son the Lord is a life-saver!

SECOND COMRADE: Mfundisi, that is not so . . .

PRIEST: My son please listen to me. I can see that you are a lost soul [*confers
with the other hostel inmates*]. Akunjalo Madoda (Is that not so gentlemen)?
Truly you are on the wrong path. You need to be saved. Come let us go
to church; and pray with me and I'll make you the fisher of men. Come,
come . . .

SECOND COMRADE: Mfundisi, can't you see what Tixo (God) has done to
us?

PRIEST: My son let us forget everything, let us just praise the Lord, hallelujah!

SECOND COMRADE: Tixo! Tixo! [*Looking up with his hands together as in
prayer and doing a mock prayer. The priest ignores him and continues to
sing.*] Do you see what you have done? I want to talk to you my Lord! I
want to talk to your cabinet. In your cabinet I want to talk to your Minister
of Labour and Manpower. O Bawo (Father)! I want to stop him from forcing
my people to live this sham life in the hostel. My Lord, in your cabinet I

want to talk to the Minister of Police . . . I want to stop him using that teargas and bullets on my people . . . !

PRIEST [*agitated*]: Niyamva madoda? Do you hear him gentlemen?

SECOND COMRADE [*continues*]: O Bawo, why don't you answer when we talk to you Tixo Wamazulu (God in heaven)?

PRIEST: My son, that is not the way to pray to the Lord. You can't just howl anything at the Lord! All you have to do is this, look I will show you. Yizani nani madoda (Come you too gentlemen). Kneel down, fold your arms and close your eyes and speak with the Lord, definitely the Lord will answer. Is that not right gentlemen? Ucabanga ukuthi bonke lababantu bayahlanya (Do you think all these people are mad)?

SECOND COMRADE: Mfundisi, that is the wrong way.

PRIEST: This is the right way . . . ?

SECOND COMRADE: But mfundisi, didn't you read in the newspaper four months ago that when children demanded the right education, they were given the dogs, bullets, and the teargas . . .

PRIEST: My son please listen to me; do you know why? It's simply because those children forgot to praise the Lord. Man must not lose patience with the Lord. God knows and sees what he's doing. Running up and down the streets shouting Amandla! Power! Power to the people is a sign of impatience! Give praise to the Lord! Give praise to his holiness! Let us praise the Lord!

SECOND COMRADE: Mfundisi listen, the workers in the factories . . .

PRIEST: Listen my son, we are not talking about workers and the factories, we are talking about God and his Bible that's all!

SECOND COMRADE: They are demanding to control the means of production and to form co-operatives. They are calling for the eradication of the land-lord system. They are now talking of the powerful People's Republic of Zanj.

PRIEST [*recalls*]: Ahaa! Young man, I suspect you of being one of the most wanted agitators . . . you are too young to be in this hostel.

SECOND COMRADE [*realises the danger*]: I don't understand what you are talking about Mfundisi . . .

PRIEST: Yes, yes, you understand what I mean. I'm seeing your face for the first time in the hostel and suddenly I get all these funny questions from you. Hayi suka kwedini (Get away young man). Suka man. Kwedini, uyandimangaza! Tyhini kwedini uyandimangaza (young man you really surprise me)! You are polluting the minds of these people.

The inmates are all surprised and suspicious. Some of them start to walk away from the two.

SECOND COMRADE: But Mfundisi . . .

PRIEST: Suka kwedini uzandifaka ezinkathazweni (you'll get me into trouble).

SECOND COMRADE [*regretfully*]: Mfundisi . . .

PRIEST: Suka mfanandini uzandibambisa (you will get me arrested)!

He exits, singing.

SECOND COMRADE: I wonder . . . Hey gentlemen do you think I went over the top? [*The inmates continue to move out as he begs them to listen to his explanations for a while.*] No madoda, I think it is right to tell him in the face rather than pretend we are happy with his preaching. [*He turns to look behind him.*] Uthini Sibanyoni? What did you say? I understand your point but I think if we don't do it now we will lose out on all this potential support of the workforce in the hostels. All right Sibanyoni, from today, I will leave you to co-operate with the priest and mobilise the hostel dwellers. I will not talk to them any more, except in our hostel block meetings. I see the danger. Gentlemen you can now go . . . enjoy yourselves.

The rest move out.

Enter FIRST COMRADE

FIRST COMRADE [*Angry*]: You've blown it!

SECOND COMRADE: Blown what?

FIRST COMRADE: What did you talk to the priest about? Why did you do it? This is dangerous. We will never be able to educate these people if we're not careful.

SECOND COMRADE: No we were talking about God.

FIRST COMRADE: You lie, this is dangerous. Ag voertsek!

Scene Four

TIME: A few weeks later

PLACE: Same hostel

CHARACTERS: The two comrades

SECOND COMRADE: Hee Mngani wam! My friend! Hee Zondabantu! [*Name*] You promised that you'd do something for me noba ayiphelelanga (even if its not in full). Come, I want it. We won't be working tomorrow!

FIRST COMRADE [*shouting back from another room*]: Ke nnete mogwera ke nale yona (Yes my friend I have it) . . .

SECOND COMRADE: Letha sizojabula (Bring it here and let's enjoy ourselves).

He goes out to him and they both come back singing and dancing.

SONG:

Nazi Bazooka Aphe Angola	There's a bazooka in Angola
Nazi Bazooka Aphe Angola	
Sizo Bashaya	We will beat them
Sizo Badubula . . .	We will shoot them . . .

They stop and hug each other excitedly.

FIRST COMRADE [*takes out a bottle of gin from his pocket*]: Šee yona ke go boditše (Here it is my compatriot, I told you)!

SECOND COMRADE: Yiza nayo nganeno (Bring it over here).

FIRST COMRADE: O a bona wena mogwera ke go rata kudu, ke be ke tla no dula ke go rata ka mokgwa o le ge nkabe o le leburu (You see compatriot, I like you, I'd still like you even if you were a boer).

They laugh

SECOND COMRADE: Uyazi mnganam (You know my friend), I feel great when I'm with you.

FIRST COMRADE: That I know! Nke o kwe mo (Taste here)!

SECOND COMRADE: What's this? Ahh Old Buck dry gin . . .

FIRST COMRADE: O bolela maaka (you lie)! It's an old friend . . . [*They laugh and drink.*] Hey, not so much! [*Snatches it.*] I know when you are drunk you have a loose tongue and that you'll start saying dangerous things. Not guntyu, guntyu, guntyu (gulp, gulp, gulp)! Nonsense. Look, just a sip. Ahh!

SECOND COMRADE: Yes iyasebenza . . . it's working!

FIRST COMRADE: Ke nnete mokgotse, e a galaka eupsa e bose (Yes compatriot, it's dry yet it's tasty).

FIRST COMRADE: E nkgopotša koša ela (It makes me think of that song) . . . [*Sings*] Ho nants bazooka Ho aphe Angola . . . come, sing . . .

They sing. FIRST COMRADE *dances. Silence.*

SECOND COMRADE: My friend, this song reminds me of those days when we canvassed together to make the students aware of the crisis of Bantu Education. Remember the days when we were running around looking for a hideout?

FIRST COMRADE [*warning*]: Ke tšeo ge [There you are]! O a thoma! You're starting again with your dangerous talk. I told you. You have a loose tongue when you are drunk. Bona mo (Look here), let me tell you this. Our honeymoon in this hostel may soon come to an end as long as we forget ourselves and keep getting excited. Look at this. [*Imitates his dancing for a split second.*] This excitement is getting dangerous. Today all those who are getting excited and running up and down the streets are being called agitators, terrorists and communists and their lives are being destroyed by this oppressive system in the prisons. Some of them face death and there is no mercy for them. Your own brothers whom you so trust may give you away, because some of them are trained to treat their people as if they were without feeling, informers! I remember now one incident of a comrade I met in the Northern Transvaal who was at home with his wife sleeping in the front room. Their children were sleeping in the back room of their two roomed shack. [*He demonstrates the scenario.*] Suddenly, the door burst open 'GQWA!!!' The cries of their children could be heard everywhere in the township. Before they even knew what was happening, four heavily armed white policemen and a black man in a balaclava, were standing right above their bed pulling the blankets off their naked bodies.

SECOND COMRADE: Awu! mfondini (man)! You mean they pulled the blankets off while he was having a foga-foga (quickie)? [*Gestures with his hand.*]

FIRST COMRADE [*slapping the hand*]: Your manners! They dragged him away from his wife. She cried and wanted to know what he had done. They told her not to worry because they would release him soon. Do you know why he was arrested?

SECOND COMRADE: No my friend . . .

FIRST COMRADE: Because he had a loose tongue when drunk, just like you. Leshilo towe (Bloody fool)! You talk too much. Blah! blah! blah!

SECOND COMRADE: Awu! My friend I get you, now you remind me of an incident I never wanted to tell you about. [*Flashback.* SECOND COMRADE *portrays an incident of an old man going to church with his wife while the* FIRST COMRADE *portrays a white policeman*]

FIRST COMRADE: Ee! Nkosikazi masiye enkonzweni (Yes wife, let's go to church). You see vrou, Jehova in the seventh heaven will bless us. Nkosikazi, u-yehova loves us all and we must praise him! Uyehova . . .

POLICEMAN [*confronting them*]: Ja julle Yehova!

OLD MAN: More bass (Morning boss).

POLICEMAN: Waarheen gaan julle Jehova (Where are you heading to)?

OLD MAN: Siya enkonzweni (We are going to church) phesheya! Phaya! That other side of the mountain.

POLICEMAN: Luister nou mooi Jehova (Listen carefully Jehova)? Kunzweni phushuphaya phushuphaya [*he deliberately distorts the language*] dan verstaan ek nie daardie taal Jehova (I don't understand that language). Toe maar Jehova, laat ons jou dompas sien (Come Jehova let's see your passbook).

OLD MAN [*searching himself, then asking the wife*]: Passbook! Nkosikazi where is my passbook? O hayi! isendlini mlungu wam (it's at home my white man).

POLICEMAN [*becoming impatient*]: Wat? Sendlwini sendlwini se voet! Jy het hom gebrand (You burned it)! You destroyed it heh? Kom, kom, kom! [*Drags him.*] My foot, you've burnt it, come, come come!

SECOND COMRADE [*relating*]: I could not stand there and watch this happen to the old man. I challenged the policeman, grabbing him by the neck. [*Demonstrates.*] Angry. Suddenly, the whole place was teeming with police. I just don't know how I escaped . . .

127

FIRST COMRADE: You see now! What would have happened if you were arrested? What would have happened to me? What would have happened to all the people who are talking about the Powerful People's Republic of Zanj? I'm warning you for the last time, you are endangering our mission!

He leaves.

Scene Five

TIME: Same day.

PLACE: Same hostel:

CHARACTERS: The same comrades

SECOND COMRADE *is sitting. He is tired and morose. Enter* FIRST COMRADE. *He carries a brazier, gauze wire and an iron and is muttering.*

FIRST COMRADE: I've been telling you one thing all the time.

He puts the brazier down, puts the wire on the brazier and the iron on top of the wire. Goes out. Comes back with a shirt on his left shoulder, carrying an ironing board. Still muttering.

FIRST COMRADE: . . . and every now and then I must tell you the same thing again. [*Realises the brazier is not burning properly. Kneels down to blow at it but is overcome with smoke. A flame comes up. He turns to his comrade who is sitting quietly on the floor.*] Tell me, why don't you respect the disciplines of our struggle? Don't you want to see the people achieve their liberation? Hai Suka man! [SECOND COMRADE *tries to respond but is immediately dismissed.*] Fuck off man!

SECOND COMRADE *goes out and returns with a small round plastic washing basin.* FIRST COMRADE *burns his hand with the iron as he tries to remove it from the fire. He jumps with pain and runs towards his fellow comrade who, thinking there is some danger somewhere, runs away too. They stop.* SECOND COMRADE *realises what has happened. He goes out and returns with some ointment to apply to his comrade's hand.*

SECOND COMRADE: What is it?

FIRST COMRADE: It's this bloody iron.

129

SECOND COMRADE [*mocking him*]:   You must learn the disciplines of ironing.

FIRST COMRADE: Shut up you bastard!

SECOND COMRADE [*giggling*]:   Daardie het jou iron reggemaak (The iron has fixed you up). Oh, I'm sorry my friend.

FIRST COMRADE: Don't be sorry; you must be careful! [*Silence. Goes to look through the window*] Comrade, the postman . . .

SECOND COMRADE [*rushing to join him at the window*]:   Comrade Postman? Let him come. Is he in his duty uniform?

FIRST COMRADE: No. You know people will start suspecting him. I hope he has some messages from the camp. Listen, you stand guard by the window and I'll close the door as soon as he's inside. You keep watch so that nobody must come inside, hear?

SECOND COMRADE *starts humming a tune about his girlfriend Nomathemba. They wait till the Postman is inside. The character of the Postman is mimed throughout the scene.*

FIRST COMRADE [*opening the door*]:   Come inside comrade.

SECOND COMRADE: Hi comrade!

FIRST COMRADE: Yes comrade. Yes. A letter? [*He opens it as* SECOND COMRADE *keeps watch by the window. He reads silently as the other sings loudly.*] Tell me comrade, when did you receive this letter? Yesterday? Good. Good.

SECOND COMRADE *starts to wash his face whilst he keeps watch, and continues singing.   He is inquisitive and keeps peeping at the letter, whereupon his colleague warns him by pushing him toward the window.*

FIRST COMRADE: You are supposed to be watching, not washing!

SECOND COMRADE: Oh, I'm sorry comrade.

FIRST COMRADE [*to the Postman*]:   Don't worry comrade, you know this one can be out of order sometimes. Now tell me comrade, does the camp want any message back? No? Good news! [*He calls out to his colleague.*] Hey listen to this . . .

BOTH [*reading*]:   'Messages received in the Camp Headquarters . . . you are to leave the hideout in two weeks' time . . .'

SECOND COMRADE [*excited*]:   In two weeks' time, in the camp yea!

FIRST COMRADE: Hey comrade, now I imagine myself in the camp . . . look at this – [*throws imaginary grenades at imaginary enemy*] blowing the enemy apart . . .

SECOND COMRADE: Hayi suka wena! Wena you'll never go to the front line . . .

FIRST COMRADE: Who told you that . . .

SECOND COMRADE: You are so thin you'll do the cooking in the camp. Jy's bloody maer . . .

FIRST COMRADE: Segaswi tena! O a gafa (Bloody mad-cap! You are mad)! Maybe it's you who will be cooking in the camp!

SECOND COMRADE [*going to look through the window*]: Comrade! Comrade . . . ?

FIRST COMRADE: What?

SECOND COMRADE: That dirty damned priest again . . .

FIRST COMRADE: Mang (Who)? Hey listen, let me go and hide the comrade. Hey, come comrade. [*He leads the Postman out.*]

From a distance the PRIEST *can be heard singing. He only starts preaching as he enters the hostel room. He sees* SECOND COMRADE.

PRIEST [*stops preaching*]: Hey young man, are you still in this hostel?

SECOND COMRADE: What did you think Mfundisi?

PRIEST: I thought you would be in jail already.

SECOND COMRADE: Listen Mfundisi, I'm leaving this hostel in two weeks' time . . .

PRIEST: I shall be very glad my son . . .

SECOND COMRADE: And when I come back, you'll do your dirty preaching outside the hostel.

PRIEST: What about my flock on cold winter days?

SECOND COMRADE: Outside the hostel.

PRIEST: Look here mfana wam. Let us not fight over nothing, uyeva? Do you hear? You mind your business and I'll mind mine. Uyabona (You see) mfana wam I've got a flock to look after in this hostel. So mfana wam, I beg you andiyifuni inkathazo (I don't want trouble).

He decides to leave as SECOND COMRADE *hurls insults at him.*

SECOND COMRADE: Hayi suka! Hamba Mfundisi . . . nja; hond! [*Left alone, he takes out a book and starts to read. He laughs.*] This guy Hadley Chase! Skelm [*Crook*]! You know in two weeks' time I'll be doing it like here in the camp! [*He stops talking to himself as he hears his colleague talking to*

131

someone. Every sentence of what his colleague says echoes in his head, in English.]

FIRST COMRADE: Hallo my groot baas.

SECOND COMRADE: Hallo my big baas.

FIRST COMRADE: Nee my groot baas ek bly hierso by Duduza Hostel.

SECOND COMRADE: No my big boss I live here at Duduza Hostel.

FIRST COMRADE: Ja groot baas.

SECOND COMRADE: Yes big boss.

FIRST COMRADE: Nee, ek steel mos nie, ek is 'n goeie man.

SECOND COMRADE: No, I don't steal, I'm a good man.

FIRST COMRADE: Nee my baas ek kom van die winkel af my baas.

SECOND COMRADE: No my boss I come from the shops my boss.

FIRST COMRADE: Ja my baas.

SECOND COMRADE: Yes my boss.

FIRST COMRADE: Wat my baas.

SECOND COMRADE: What my boss.

FIRST COMRADE: My naam is Zondabantu. Maar jy kan my sommer Zondi noem . . . dis maklikker vir you.

SECOND COMRADE: My name is Zondabantu. [*Aside*] I know you white people can't pronounce black people's names; you can simply call me Zondi . . . it is easier for you.

FIRST COMRADE: Ja baas, wat my baas?

SECOND COMRADE: Yes boss, what my boss?

FIRST COMRADE: My dompas?

SECOND COMRADE: My passbook?

FIRST COMRADE: Nee my baas, ek het hom. Hy's hierso by die hostel met 'n stamp aan my baas . . .

SECOND COMRADE: No my boss, I have it. It's here in the hostel, valid with a stamp my boss . . . [*Aside*] Keep him at a distance. And remember to keep smiling [*smiles*].

FIRST COMRADE: Ja my groot baas.

SECOND COMRADE: Yes my big boss.

FIRST COMRADE: Wat nou my baas – daarso by jou kom?

SECOND COMRADE: What now my boss, come to you? [*Aside*] Now is the time to run away . . .

FIRST COMRADE: Aowa lo a gafa . . .

SECOND COMRADE: You are mad!

FIRST COMRADE *runs into the hostel room where his colleague jumps with fear. They rush to bolt the door.*

SECOND COMRADE: What is it? What happened?

FIRST COMRADE: It's these stupid people, the police.

SECOND COMRADE: Hee mfondini, how did they know we are here.

FIRST COMRADE [*terrified*]: I don't know.

SECOND COMRADE: I'm telling you it's that damn priest. [*They peep through the window.*]

FIRST COMRADE: No. It's not the priest . . .

SECOND COMRADE: It's him.

FIRST COMRADE: It's not the priest.

SECOND COMRADE [*grabbing him by the shirt*]: My friend, when I come back from the camp, I'll squeeze the shit out of him!

FIRST COMRADE: No man, you don't have to squeeze the shit out of me!

SECOND COMRADE: Sorry. Anyway, didn't they see the comrade?

FIRST COMRADE: No. These ones know nothing about State Security. All they know is to harass innocent people about the bloody dompas . . . and those who fail to produce will spend a few days in jail – bloody stupid.

BOTH: Nabaya! There they are! Voertsek!

SECOND COMRADE: Honde!

FIRST COMRADE: Stupid!

SECOND COMRADE: Zinja!

FIRST COMRADE: Hey they are stopping! [*They creep away and remain still for a while and come back to poke fun at the police.*] Voertsek!

SECOND COMRADE: Na Kunya (You'll shit)!

FIRST COMRADE: Ni ya Geza Makwendini (You silly boys)!

SECOND COMRADE: Fools!

FIRST COMRADE: Hey they are stopping again. [*They creep away and then decide to stop the fun.*]

SECOND COMRADE [*going to the window*]: Hamba! Nja! Hond! Julle moer! Nda 'ni fumana ngenyi'mini! One day I'll go over there I get my bazooka and I'll shoot you to pieces . . .

FIRST COMRADE: Hey! No man! No! Have you got a bazooka? Uyabona, you see, we are acting like amateurs. Remember, we are supposed to be in the camp in five days time not in jail. Imagine being arrested now when we are left with only five days. Hayi man my friend jy moet dink. You must think.

SECOND COMRADE [*regretfully*]: You are right my friend, but these people are provocative . . .

FIRST COMRADE: Hayi man tlogela batho bao! (Leave those people alone)!

He takes out the newspaper and starts reading. His colleague continues with his novel. Silence.

SECOND COMRADE: Anyway, what's interesting in your paper today?

FIRST COMRADE: Bus fares are up, people are crying.

SECOND COMRADE: Ag shame and then . . .

FIRST COMRADE [*reading*]: 'There is an increase in house rent . . .' Look, listen to this – ' . . . it started three months ago and when the residents demanded an explanation the authorities said "we're sorry we can't do anything about it" . . .'

SECOND COMRADE: Bastards! En toe?

FIRST COMRADE: Shuu my friend, everything is going up-up-up. Sales Tax e ile godimo ke 20 per cent (is increased to 20 per cent). And now the poor are the hardest hit.

SECOND COMRADE: I hate that. We have no reason to maintain this system with its corrupt ministers. They must go and retrieve that money from Rhoodie. The clever bastard . . . Former Minister of Information, he steals R8 million from the department, takes it into Swiss banks, tells the government that if they charge him, he will reveal the names of all the other untouchables and they withdraw the threat. Shit man! Jammer ou Vorster is dood (Pity old Vorster is dead].

Pause.

FIRST COMRADE: Hey, listen. It seems your secret visit to the Eastern Cape has worked.

SECOND COMRADE: You say so. But I was nearly caught.

FIRST COMRADE: Forget about being caught man. Listen to this, '. . . in the Eastern Cape school children are embarking on a boycott which they say will spiral to other parts of the country. They say this is a different kind of boycott . . . to spread the ABC of Education for the Dispossessed.'

SECOND COMRADE [*boastfully*]: Jaa! my friend, it's those boys from the school I started with. If those boys went to the camp today they would make good cadres. The boys and girls from Tembalethu High School have the courage and the tact. Hawu Pambili 'Zwelinzima. Now they understand the ABC of the Education for the Dispossessed.

FIRST COMRADE: . . . Hey, but eighty-seven were killed.

SECOND COMRADE: Eighty-seven?

FIRST COMRADE: '. . . And one-eighty-nine were detained. Policemen used guns, bullets, dogs and the sneeze machine . . . 'Now the whole land is overshadowed by an ugly cloud . . . '

SECOND COMRADE [*a mock prayer*]: Awu Tixo, hayi ke khawuze uzo ku-thetha ngukwakhu nalama bhulu (Oh God, now you must come in person to talk to the boers)! My Lord what are you waiting for? We know it's comfortable for you up there! Come down for a minute and see for yourself what is happening down here. Siyanya ngalamabhulu kweli cala lase mhla-beni Bawo (The boers make us shit this side of the earth)! Oh! my Lord Khawusithumele nathi okwethu – iAK47 (Send us something of our own – the AK47)! Ne (and) handgrenades. Don't forget i-bazooka bawo. Oh my Lord sithumele nathi i-teargas – nathi sifuna ukubanyisa ngoku khawuleza bawo (We too want to make them shit)! Yes Bawo, come in person with the limpet mines. Ungalamuli xa sesibanyisa nathi Bawo. Don't stand in the way of our triumph when we have our feet on their faces!

FIRST COMRADE: Hey! Hey! Remember I was in the Northern Transvaal two days ago?

SECOND COMRADE: Yes.

FIRST COMRADE: Now listen to this, 'the whole Northern Transvaal work-force is on strike; and thousands in other areas are beginning to march to the cities'. [SECOND COMRADE *portrays the march with the soft humming of a revolutionary song in the background – siyaya . . . siyaya.*] They no longer demand higher wages. They now demand to form co-operatives, a word unknown to South Africa. Trade unions in the north, south and west have indicated that they will follow the steps taken by their colleagues in the Northern Transvaal pending their colleagues' decision on 'Revolt or

135

Reform'. Security Intelligence Agency suspect it may be the work of infiltrators and agitators. A man-hunt is on to bring these to book.' They are crazy; it's millions! It's not just a few people.

SECOND COMRADE: We've got them. A soze basifumane (They'll never find us).

FIRST COMRADE: Re ba swere ka fase. We have got them by the balls. The message is spreading like wild fire. [*Laughs.*] This is our message to the future liberated Powerful People's Republic of Zanj . . . [*The following sections are addressed to the audience.*] First, the worker must understand that by co-operatives we mean co-operative farming structures and mining industries . . .

SECOND COMRADE: Co-operatives can work in the rural areas, in the villages and in the cities where technology is highly advanced. We cannot afford to have the wealth of our country belonging to only a few who do not care for the people who are responsible for the production. Co-operatives would mean the employment of millions resulting in high production!

FIRST COMRADE: Co-operative irrigation schemes shall be examples of developing arid lands where our people have been relegated to starve to death. The people's government shall initiate and maintain these schemes!

SECOND COMRADE: So that everybody shall be able to supply whatever needs they are faced with.

FIRST COMRADE: And my people, the greater population would sense that working together will benefit all the dispossessed!

BOTH [*facing each other, both hands on each other's shoulders*]: We must form communes, groups of people living together, sharing properties and responsibilities, and there will be no room for poverty and hunger; no room for capitalism in the Powerful People's Republic of Zanj!

FIRST COMRADE [*returning to the newspaper*]: Hey listen to this . . . 'Three different unions in the newly formed Homeland Union Federation of KwaZulu, who are opposed to Congress, have appealed to the international world through their homeland leader for the recognition of their Homeland Union.' Tixo! Ka (of) Ntsikane!

SECOND COMRADE: Tixo Ka Sekhukhune no (and) Ma-Ngoyi. Tixo Ka Sobukwe no Mandela. My God! But these people are fighting a different battle!

FIRST COMRADE: Ag man, batho ba ba a gafa, they are mad, together with their leader. Le re ba lwelang bjale (What is their fight all about)? All right, tell me people, if they are fighting for the international recognition of their homeland union are they aware that the homelands are a creation of the same oppressive system, and an attempt to deny the oppressed masses their rightful claim to their land. Or, are they openly fighting for the maintenance of the same corrupt system with the difference that their leaders should be restored to power? They are mad, baagafa. Together with their leader.

SECOND COMRADE: What about the millions in those drought stricken rural areas?

BOTH: If you play with people beware, because people can react!
Laughter and celebration.

Scene Six

TIME: The Following day.

PLACE: Same hostel

SECOND COMRADE: Comrade, remember the trip to the camp is in only five days' time?

FIRST COMRADE: Yes comrade.

SECOND COMRADE: Is it perhaps not important to have our passports ready in case . . .

FIRST COMRADE: What are you talking about now? There is no chance of us getting passports unless we want to be arrested.

SECOND COMRADE: I have investigated it. There is very little danger . . .

FIRST COMRADE: I don't understand you.

SECOND COMRADE: Let us go to Ciskei . . .

FIRST COMRADE: Oh yes, I can disguise myself as a priest and we can get our passports in one day. You know those fools there truly think they are independent . . .

SECOND COMRADE: This is the only time in my life that I agree to go to that homeland and make those fools feel legitimate.

FIRST COMRADE: I will disguise as priest. Now wait here for me . . .

SECOND COMRADE [recalling]: Priest? He knows I hate priests. Why should he choose to become a priest? We'll see.

FIRST COMRADE returns with a blazer and a priest's collar and spectacles. He changes clothes on stage to the amazement of SECOND COMRADE.

SECOND COMRADE [stunned]: Hau comrade priest!

FIRST COMRADE: Now comrade, tell me, do I look like a priest?

SECOND COMRADE: You look like eh – Bishop . . . Bishop . . .

FIRST COMRADE: Tutu!

SECOND COMRADE: No man, you look like ehn . . . Bishop Muzorewa.

FIRST COMRADE: Ag shit! Anyway if it does the trick why worry?

SECOND COMRADE: Now you wait here for a while.

FIRST COMRADE [*talking to himself*]: Bishop Muzorewa . . .?

SECOND COMRADE *returns with an old hat, a stick and an old coat and starts to dress up.* FIRST COMRADE *is impressed.*

FIRST COMRADE: Well my friend, you look like an old pensioner. [*Pause. They laugh.*] Well, we are ready, what are we waiting for?

BOTH: Siyaya e-Ciskei (We'll march to Ciskei)!

Scene Seven

TIME: Morning

CHARACTERS: SECOND COMRADE as an OLD MAN throughout the scene. FIRST COMRADE plays the priest, the passport official and MR NDLOVU. The priest later becomes imaginary. The watchman is imaginary.

PLACE: Ciskei Passport Office.

A number of people are waiting outside the office gate. They sound a little impatient as the time for opening has long passed. A watchman is keeping an eye on the behaviour of the people.

OLD MAN: Watchman please open the gate! I have come to collect my passport, it's getting late already.

PRIEST: Oh come on now, 'Watchie', open up man!

OLD MAN: I am going to miss my bus home 'Watchie', it's late!

PRIEST: I'm invited overseas to the Bishop's Conference 'Watchie'! Ja . . . Ja!

OLD MAN: All right 'Watchie'. Please, 'Watchie' . . . It's almost eight o'clock! Open the gate!

The gate is opened and numbers of people flock inside the yard whereupon they are made to stand in a queue. FIRST COMRADE goes backstage to play MR NDLOVU.

OLD MAN [*to the* WATCHMAN]: Mister Ndlovu is waiting for me inside . . . Ja. [*laughs*] Yes Watchman. It's true. Ja I've come to collect my passport. Ja. Thank you Watchman. [*People start to push as everyone wants to be at the front of the queue. He calls out.*] Mister Ndlovu . . . !

A voice comes from somewhere at the back.

MR NDLOVU: Hey Voertsek! Voertsek man! Stop calling my name!

140

OLD MAN: These people are pushing, Mister Ndlovu! [*Silence.*] Mister Ndlovu . . . ! These people won't stop pushing, Mister Ndlovu!

OLD MAN [*appealing to everyone]:* People stop pushing man! People, can't you see umfundisi? Yes priest . . . you are right. [*To the imaginary priest.*] Stand to one side. These people have no manners mfundisi.

Enter MR NDLOVU *in a white dustcoat and whistling.*

MR NDLOVU: Yes, yes one line and no pushing! One line! [*Inspects them closely.*] Yes Priest, can't you see the queue? What? Invited overseas? That is not my business, my business is the queue. Back to the queue, hamba, hamba! Hei nina, (you) move back and stop pushing otherwise I'll send you back home. C'mon, back! [*Pushes them backwards*] Back! And stop pushing or you'll have to come back tomorrow.

He goes into his office and calls them in one by one.

MR NDLOVU: First one! . . . You are from Cape Town? C'mon, outside. Next one! Dompas? [*Looks at document.*] Hei you are from Port Elizabeth? Outside. Next one! Your dompas? You are from Grahamstown. Outside. Bamba phuma ngapha! Stupid! Next one! Dompas? Hei, you are from East London? Bamba apha and outside! [*He goes out angrily.*] Hei listen! All those who are from Cape Town, Port Elizabeth, Johannesburg, Grahamstown, one side! [*He hurries them up.*] C'mon, move! Move, move mamma, yiza, yiza, yiza (come, come, come)! Hei wena voertsek oneside. Hei Priest, what is it? Nine o'clock flight? Come here. [*Puts him in the front of the queue.*] Hei wena don't push; this is a priest. Back! [*Pushes them backwards.*] Don't push the mfundisi!

OLD MAN: Yes Mister Ndlovu!

MR NDLOVU: Baphelele? Hei wena kom hierso laat ek jou dompas sien? Kom blaai om. [*Looks at it suspiciously.*] Ek sê mos jy kom van Vrystaat. Haak Vrystaat! Move! Right, [*to the* PRIEST] Bishop's Conference kom laat ons jou dompas sien (let's see your passbook). [*The* PRIEST *produces it as the* OLD MAN *strains his neck to look into the document.*] Hey uqavile old man, you are too inquisitive. Page through, mfundisi, page some more. That's it . . . priest, you are taking chances. You do not qualify for this homeland. Hayi man yiza yiza mfundisi. What? Listen mfundisi, I beg you, don't beg me please mfundisi. Yiza hamba man mfundisi! What? Money? I'm sorry mfundisi I don't take bribes. Hamba, go mfundisi! [*To the others.*] Baphelele? [*The* PRIEST *kneels down to pray.*] No. No mfundisi, this is no time for prayers. Go! Baphelele?

OLD MAN: Ewe (Yes) Mister Ndlovu...

MR NDLOVU: Hey shut your big mouth wena! Baphelele? [*Looks about.*] Baphelele?

OLD MAN: I was trying to...

MR NDLOVU: Voertsek! Shut up! Baphelele? [*Silence*] Now listen to me all of you. [*Referring to those standing on the one side.*] Mamelani nonke (Listen all), you go back to your government and you tell them that I say mina Ndlovu that 'they must stop buying a lot of police equipment. They must also worry about their people's travelling problems.'
Siyevana (Do we agree)? Sivene (Do we agree)?

The OLD MAN *stays, waving his hand to bid them farewell as they leave. He seems content with the fact that there won't be more pushing.*

MR NDLOVU: Hei old man, you are so inquisitive. Where do you come from?

OLD MAN: Oh, I am a beautiful Ciskeian.

MR NDLOVU: Uzube kanti uyaxoka (I hope you are not telling lies)!

OLD MAN: No. I've got my document...

MR NDLOVU: Uzube Kanti uyaxoka!

OLD MAN:... And my identity.

MR NDLOVU: Uyakunya (You'll shit)!

OLD MAN: No Mister Ndlovu. Angixoki. I'm not lying.

MR NDLOVU: Ngena. Inside! [*The* OLD MAN *enters*] Dompas? Permit? [*The* OLD MAN *fiddles through his coat.*] Hey, I haven't got the whole day here. You are wasting my time...

OLD MAN:... There you are, Mister Ndlovu...

The telephone rings and MR NDLOVU *picks it up.*

MR NDLOVU: Hallo! Just hold on a minute please. [*He sends the* OLD MAN *outside.*] Hei phuma voertsek! Phuma (Out)! Hallo! Oh, good morning to you, Mr Hannekom... I'm fine thank you. Ja... Ja, who's that? Reverend Muzorewa? [*The* OLD MAN *comes closer to the door to eavesdrop on the conversation.*] Now tell me, Mr Hannekom, is he any relation to the bishop in Zimbabwe? [*Laughs*] Ja... Ja... Anyway, Mr Hannekom, I've already seen the Reverend. Yes, you know Mr. Hannekom, there is no chance of fixing his documents without going back to the South African authorities... Yes. Ja... you know we've had lots of problems with the South African authorities about such cases in the past. I'm sorry Mr. Hannekom I can't help in this case ... Send him back to the South African authorities. Yes. Alright, goodbye! [*Drops the phone.*] O, that priest is trying to be clever hey, we'll meet somewhere. [*Calls out to the old man.*] Bhekinja?

OLD MAN: Mister Ndlovu?

MR NDLOVU [*demanding*]: Dompas?

OLD MAN: I gave you ...

MR NDLOVU: Permit?

OLD MAN: There it is ...

MR NDLOVU: Lodger's card. [OLD MAN *fiddles.*] Hey I haven't got the whole day here. [*He takes it.*] UIF card?

OLD MAN: May I go out and ask my wife?

MR NDLOVU: I said I haven't got the whole day here.

OLD MAN [*finding it*]: I knew I had it ... [*laughs*].

MR NDLOVU [*writing down the information*]: Death certificate?

OLD MAN [*perplexed*]: Mister Ndlovu?

MR NDLOVU [*impatient*]: Death certificate? I haven't got the whole day here ...

OLD MAN [*can't believe his ears and inspects his body*]: But Mister Ndlovu, I'm still alive.

MR NDLOVU [*shouting angrily in his face*]: It's all this crazy set up here that drives me mad. Is julle wat my deurmekaar maak. Passport photos?

OLD MAN: There you are ...

MR NDLOVU *compares all the documents and leaves for a brief while. He returns and calls out softly to the* OLD MAN.

MR NDLOVU: Do you see that paper?

OLD MAN: Yes, Mr Ndlovu.

MR NDLOVU: Now listen carefully. You've got to do something noba ayi-phelelelanga (even if it's just a little). Otherwise you'll get your passport in six months time.

OLD MAN: Oh no, my son ...

MR NDLOVU: Hey you call me your son?

OLD MAN: No ... I say sir ... You know sir, I've only got ten rands in my pocket. [*He puts the money in* MR NDLOVU'*s coat pocket.*]

MR NDLOVU [*going to the door*]: Hey watchman, you close the gate. I am on lunch now. I am taking no more cases. Okay [*to the* OLD MAN] you'll get your passport next week, hear? Goodbye.

OLD MAN: But Mister Ndlovu, I'm leaving tomorrow. Hawu please Mister Ndlovu. [*He tries to explain*] Mister Ndlovu you know...

MR NDLOVU: Shut up! Voertsek man. [*Pause*] Do you know where I live?

OLD MAN: Yes Mister Ndlovu.

MR NDLOVU: Do you know how many dogs I have? Are you not scared of dogs?

OLD MAN: Oh no Mister Ndlovu, I like dogs. You know Mister Ndlovu, forty years ago when I was a young boy here in Ciskei, I used to hunt hares and rabbits with dogs. Dogs are my best friends, Mister Ndlovu.

MR NDLOVU: Now you come to my home tonight at seven o'clock. Listen, you bring another twenty rands, do you hear me.

OLD MAN: For sure Mister Ndlovu, I'll do that, Mister Ndlovu.

MR NDLOVU: Goodbye!

OLD MAN: All right Mister Ndlovu, you are a good man! You serve your people well! Au Mister Ndlovu, I'll tell my wife about you! [*Laughs and takes off the disguise.*] Straight to 'the camp' in Libya tomorrow!

Scene Eight

TIME: Evening

PLACE: Hostel

CHARACTERS: The two comrades, police

FIRST COMRADE *walks dejectedly, into the room with the jacket in his hand. Sits down.* SECOND COMRADE *comes in, excitedly singing the 'bazooka' song. He carries two heavy suitcases.*

SECOND COMRADE: I saw you had problems . . .

FIRST COMRADE: I tried another liberal in town but later I thought it could be risky, so I phoned him to drop the plans.

SECOND COMRADE [*mocking*]: Now my friend, do you want to try again?

FIRST COMRADE: What?

SECOND COMRADE: What about those funny glasses on your face?

FIRST COMRADE *throws them away.* SECOND COMRADE *lights a candle.*

SECOND COMRADE: Comrade do not worry. There are many ways to leave this country. Ndiyakuxelela, uzakuthubeleza (I tell you, you will skip). This is your land! No one else knows it better than you. Remember the old man's words: Only when people are desperate, do they become brave. My flight is tomorrow at 12 o'clock . . .

FIRST COMRADE: I'll cross the border tomorrow night. I'll meet you in two days? In 'the camp' in Libya.

SECOND COMRADE [*encouragingly*]: Hau, that's my comrade!

BOTH [*clasping hands*]: Ilizwe lelethu! Courage, the land is ours!

FIRST COMRADE: Anyway, it is getting late. Let us go to bed.

SECOND COMRADE *sings his popular Nomathemba song louder and louder . . .*

FIRST COMRADE: Hey comrade! Hey Comrade! Hayi man, lala (No man, sleep).

SECOND COMRADE: But Nomathemba is my wife . . .

FIRST COMRADE: Hayi suka man, lala, sleep man.

SECOND COMRADE *remains silent for a while and then starts humming again.*

FIRST COMRADE [*irritated*]: Hey, blow out that candle and sleep.

They sleep. FIRST COMRADE *has nightmares.* SECOND COMRADE *shouts at him to keep quiet but the nightmares continue.* SECOND COMRADE *lights the candle and kicks* FIRST COMRADE *hard so that he wakes up.*

FIRST COMRADE [*looking petrified*]: I'm sorry comrade; it's a dream . . .

SECOND COMRADE: A dream? What's wrong with a dream? Hayi man, lala.

FIRST COMRADE: This one was a strange dream . . .

SECOND COMRADE: A strange dream? Hmm . . .

FIRST COMRADE: My friend, I dreamt we were already in 'the camp' in Libya . . .

SECOND COMRADE: Wait a moment . . . Yibambe apho Kanye (Hold it just there)! You see, if your dreams are going to go as far as Libya while you are still in this country, you'll shit! In this country you must not even be suspected of dreaming about Libya. You can't afford such a dream here.

FIRST COMRADE: But it's just a dream . . .

SECOND COMRADE: I know but . . . [*feeling unsettled, he goes to peep through the window, sees a figure in the dark and calls out to his colleague*] yiza apha (Come here). Woza la! There are policemen outside. Look there. Who's that man over there?

FIRST COMRADE: That's the night-watchman. [*Taunting him.*] Hello Watchie, Watchie! Muyeke ulele. Leave him he sleeps. My friend, we were already in 'the camp' in Libya. Dressed in heavy uniform, fully trained as cadres. Ready for the first assignment. We were standing in rows with other more than one thousand comrades. There was this hefty tall middle-age field-marshall who was walking up and down the rows, singing the last instructions. He was also saying as if possessed by the spirit of our forefathers, 'Phambili makwedini! Phambili! Phambili ngo mzabalazo (struggle)! Forward with the African people's struggle! Lelenu elolizwe lilweleni! That is your land, fight for it! Mali phalale igazi lomcinezeli! Let the blood of the oppressor flow! Forward with the powerful People's Republic of Zanj!'

146

Then suddenly, there were these huge elephants that burst into the camp. The comrades started firing indiscriminately at the wild animals. I was so terrified I couldn't even raise my bazooka. Then suddenly one elephant, 'boom', fell on me. None of the comrades could see me or hear my cries as they marched out of the camp to free my country from the oppressive monster . . . *There is a loud bang on the door followed by several more bangs. The door finally breaks down and torches start to flicker exposing the two half-naked bodies of the* COMRADES. *Enter the* POLICE. *In this scene there is no order of speech as the comrades are interrogated randomly.*

SECOND COMRADE [*jumping up to go to the door*]:   Good night Sergeant! Why do you burst in like this?

FIRST COMRADE [*courageously*]:   But Sergeant, this is an ungodly hour to come and bang the door like this in somebody else's house. This is unfair . . . no man . . . !

SECOND COMRADE: We would have opened the door for you Sergeant. Nyani (True). Ja. Other people? Ja. They are on leave . . .

FIRST COMRADE: Nee, hulle is nie hier nie (they are not here) . . .

SECOND COMRADE: They are in Ciskei, Malawi, Transkei, Maputo all over the country.

FIRST COMRADE: Nee ons het geslaap. Eintlik ek het geslaap (we were asleep. Actually I was asleep). Nou hierdie man hy dream by my (Now this man dreams at me) – [*he deliberately distorts the language*], ek dream nie ek nie (I don't dream).

SECOND COMRADE: Hayi Musuqokisela umlungu (Don't tell the white man lies). Nee baas, he can't speak Afrikaans. I will tell you what happened Sergeant. You see we were fast asleep and then the dreams were rolling and rolling around his head . . .

FIRST COMRADE [*arguing with him*]:   O se ke wa bolela maaka ka nna (Don't lie about me)! Wat? Daardie sakke (Those bags)? Akusezam! Hulle is nie my sakke nie. They are not mine.

SECOND COMRADE: Hulle is myne my baas (They are mine, boss). I keep my clothes in them. You see there are no wardrobes here. No Sergeant we are going nowhere. We like this place . . .

FIRST COMRADE: For instance look we are the only two people left here, we'll die here Sergeant. Wat my baas? My naam? my naam is Zondabantu. Ek kom van baca-plek (I come from bacaland). e-Transkei.

147

SECOND COMRADE: Me. My name is Mthuthuzeli Khisimusi my baas. I come from Ndebeleland . . .

BOTH: Thina? On a wanted list?

FIRST COMRADE: No, no, no. They are mistaken . . .

SECOND COMRADE: Hayi. Niphosile (You are mistaken).

FIRST COMRADE: What now? [*He refers to a photograph shown to him.*] A-a- I've never seen that man. Ek ken hom nie my baas (I don't know him).

SECOND COMRADE: Hayi I don't know that chap. That one. No! andimyazi. Even the other one – Hayi!

FIRST COMRADE: Ek weet nie daardie mense (I don't know those people). Yintoni buti (What's wrong brother)? Yintoni? Hayi suka, my name is not Mayibuye tyini. My name is Zondabantu. Undibethela'ntoni. Why do you slap me? For saying I don't know those people? Meneer sê my nou? Waarvoor slaan hy my nou? Waarvoor (Sir tell me why is this man beating me)? . . . Now you want to force me to say that's me on that photo. I tell him I come from Transkei and he beats me. Hayi suka . . .

BOTH: What? We are being arrested for a political dream?

FIRST COMRADE: Yoo! This country has mad laws!

SECOND COMRADE: But serious Sergeant, it was just a dream. Of course we were not discussing politics.

FIRST COMRADE: Hayi, niemand gaan my slaan nie. Nobody will lay their hands on me. My ma hoor my. I swear upon my mother.

SECOND COMRADE: No baas. You can't beat me baas. I'm a sick man. . . . I've been in hospital for five years. Cancer my baas. *The police start to assault them. Dogs are let loose to bite them. There is pandemonium. Then suddenly . . .*

BOTH [*in disbelief*]: What? The Camp? In Libya. No! No!

Realising they cannot escape, the COMRADES *decide to fight back, punching and hitting with their suitcases. They are finally defeated, handcuffed and marched into the cars waiting outside. They march with the confidence of an undefeated people.*

BOTH: As we march to the prison walls, remember that we have played our role in the struggle! Now it is your turn to turn around and look at yourself!

SECOND COMRADE: Jika uzi jonge (Turn around)!

FIRST COMRADE: Tsoga o thenyake.